RHYTHMIC GYMNASTICS

The Skills of the Game

Rhythmic gymnastics is one aspect of the world of gymnastics which may not be readily known to everyone. This form of gymnastics embraces the grace and beauty of the dancer as well as the strength and agility of the gymnast, and because it involves the manipulation of hand apparatus it also requires the dexterity of the juggler, especially at the highest levels of performance.

Jenny Bott has been one of the driving forces in the development of rhythmic gymnastics in Great Britain. As well as being an outstanding coach at the highest international level, she is also a teacher. She excels in both areas, where her technical knowledge, imagination and creativity have brought much enjoyment to gymnasts, teachers and coaches at all levels.

It is in her role as the teacher that this most welcome text has been written. It is an exciting addition to the physical education curriculum and what Jenny has done so effectively is to make rhythmic gymnastics sound exciting, yet within the capabilities of all teachers, whatever their background in gymnastics.

This relatively basic text is aimed at teachers in schools and gives ideas for class work, group work and partner work all built on the basic skills. For the teachers and enthusiasts who wish to go a little further, it adds more advanced ideas.

Jenny is to be congratulated on a much needed text. All of us in physical education can now bring another exciting form of movement to children of all levels of ability.

Alma Thomas
Head of School of Human Movement Studies, Bedford College of Higher Education

If there is one person above all others who has been responsible for the development of rhythmic gymnastics in Great Britain, that person must be Jenny Bott. Not only is she Chairman of the Rhythmic Gymnastics Committee of the British Amateur Gymnastics Association but she is a national coach and has held both positions since the inception of rhythmic gymnastics in this country fifteen years ago. All this incidentally, in a totally voluntary capacity.

Jenny's depth of experience, her enthusiasm and her professional background – she is a senior lecturer in charge of the Gymnastics Department at Bedford College of Higher Education – have equipped her admirably to write this book which provides for prospective teachers and gymnasts an excellent introduction to rhythmic gymnastics and a most useful description of basic skills, including the compilation of simple exercises.

As President of the British Amateur Gymnastics Association I can, without reservation, commend this well-conceived and informative book for beginners.

Franklyn Edmonds OBE, DMA
President, British Amateur Gymnastics Association
Vice-President, International Gymnastics Federation

RHYTHMIC GYMNASTICS

The Skills of the Game

JENNY BOTT

THE CROWOOD PRESS

First published in 1989 by
The Crowood Press
Ramsbury, Marlborough,
Wiltshire SN8 2HE

British Library Cataloguing in Publication Data

Bott, Jenny
  Rhythmic gymnastics: the skills of the game.
  1. Rhythmic gymnastics
  I. Title
  796.4'1

ISBN 1-85223-208-0

Dedicated to my husband Geoff and sons David and Mark for their support and encouragement.

Acknowledgements

Thanks to gymnasts Lisa Black and Estha Jones for their time and patience in posing for the photographs, and to Ken Roberts for taking, developing and printing the photographs.

DEC 26 '90

Typeset by Keyboard Services, Luton
Printed in Great Britain by The Bath Press

Contents

1 History

Health, fitness, skill, confidence, elegance and poise are among the benefits to be derived from rhythmic gymnastics which can be enjoyed by all participants, whether children or adults. With these factors in mind, this book aims to promote participation by giving a variety of skills for the newcomer to practise and master, and also more challenging elements for the accomplished gymnast to attempt.

As such, I hope that this book will be of value to both the aspiring performer and the teacher or coach. I am asked many questions about the sport (the facilities, apparatus, music, awards, competitions, displays etc) particularly by teachers, and I hope that most of the answers will be found within this text.

Fig 1 The rope was one of the first pieces of apparatus to be recognised.

Fig 2 The hoop and the ball were given official recognition at the 1963 World Championships.

ORIGINS

The 'movement foundations' of rhythmic gymnastics originated as long ago as the early 1900s in Germany and France, but the specific rules and conditions which now govern the sport did not come into being until 1962. It was then that the International Gymnastics Federation gave official recognition to the various apparatus exercises – the rope, the hoop and the ball – and set up the first World Championships which were held in 1963. Not until some time later were the clubs and the ribbon events included.

Since 1963, the World Championships have been held every alternate year, this being the major competition in the international calendar for rhythmic gymnastics. Gradually, other competitions have been introduced: European Championships were inaugurated in 1978, and then a 'Four-Continents Championship', but the ultimate recognition for the sport was its inclusion in the Olympic Games for the first time in Los Angeles 1984 and again in Seoul in 1988.

Fig 3   The clubs represent a newer and more difficult piece of apparatus.

OLYMPIC GAMES

Current rules state that no more than two gymnasts per country are eligible for the Olympics, and that qualification is necessary before entry into the competition is allowed. The qualifying competition is a 'sudden death' affair, just one chance in the World Championships preceding the Olympic Games (usually about one year in advance), when gymnasts who reach the required standard qualify for a place to represent their country. The 'required standard' is seemingly not quite established yet, since for Los Angeles the top fifty gymnasts were eligible for qualification, while the number was increased to fifty-six for the Games

Fig 4   The ribbon was the last piece to be given official recognition.

at Seoul. On neither occasion was the decision made until after the World Championships had been held.

The group exercise has not found its way into the Olympics. With the promotion of the Olympic champion ideal, it is less likely that a team event will establish itself.

DEVELOPMENT IN THE UNITED KINGDOM

Since its inception in the United Kingdom in 1974, there has been much progress in all aspects of rhythmic gymnastics, and in recent years new ideas have developed which have made the sport more interesting, more challenging and more demanding in terms of standards and expectations.

I was honoured and privileged to be the person whom the Gymnastics Association approached in 1974 to initiate the sport and develop it in the United Kingdom. In these fifteen years, as it has become established, the sport has changed dramatically, not just in the United Kingdom but abroad as well.

Today's lifestyle is becoming more and more fitness dominated, and a healthy approach to life, be it through diet, exercise, or relaxation, is being seen as of vital importance. With changes in employment trends and the building of sports centres and leisure complexes, an awareness of the advantages and need for leisure activities is ever-growing. Already, children are being encouraged to participate in health-related fitness programmes, since they are becoming increasingly important in schools today. Along with some of the newer minority sports and activities health-related exercises

Fig 5   Opportunities for gymnasts to participate in a group event are available at most levels.

3

are included in school physical education programmes, particularly for children in the 11–16 years age range.

Here, too, we are seeing the introduction of rhythmic gymnastics, though this is spreading into primary and middle schools also. There was a time when children instigated their own playtime games in school, and they were great fun. As youngsters, we could not wait until morning break to get out and play 'dibs', 'two-balls', 'hula-hoop', 'salt, mustard, vinegar, pepper', and various other games with hoops, balls, and ropes etc. These were all games involving dexterity, co-ordination and control of small equipment, and though today's free-time activities played by children are more sophisticated and mature, the fun and games of some thirty or forty years ago are seemingly coming back, in part, in the form of rhythmic gymnastics.

Development in Schools

Young children love to play with toys and games – it is part of growing up and of learning. Equally, older children enjoy the challenge of learning and mastering intricate physical skills, and they enjoy working with friends to create and practise these skills and tricks.

School plays a major part in giving children a variety of experiences and challenges. Opportunities to participate in rhythmic gymnastics are increasing all the time. Two distinct advantages which the sport has over many others are that it can be either recreational or competitive, and it can be individual or group-oriented, so satisfying varying demands.

Despite the move away from the competitive element in schools today, it must be realised that life itself is highly competitive, and as such it is difficult to protect the child and keep him away from a competitive environment. However, this choice can be left to the teacher and pupil. Participation can be purely for fun, or can be used as a mechanism for the promotion of fitness, and it will certainly play a part in the development of social and psychological aspects in addition to the improvement of an individual's skill level. When striving to improve personal performance, the individual levels of skill and achievement are measurable in the form of an awards scheme. Here, tests of body-movement skills and apparatus-handling techniques, plus combined elements, encourage children to collect badges and certificates to show their proficiency in the sport.

There is an opportunity to compete both on an individual and team basis and in the last two years a schools' competition has been introduced which allows for competition between schools within the various regions in the United Kingdom. This culminates in a grand final when the winning schools for the various age groups in each region meet each other.

Other major competitions in Great Britain include the British Championships for Seniors and Juniors, involving both individual and group events, the Individual Apparatus Championships and inter-regional competitions and, in 1989, a new national grading structure. This is a progressive scheme for gymnasts who can begin to compete as early as eight years of age, and work their way through a competitive structure either as an élite gymnast or as a recreational gymnast, or as both. There are opportunities to compete as an individual gymnast, or with a partner, or in a trio, with the early stages taking place at club level before moving on to regional or national level.

Opportunities for coaching, judging and competing are many and varied – a mark of

Fig 6   Duet working together in movement but with different apparatus.

the progress over the last fifteen years, and also a healthy sign for the future.

Current Trends

I would suggest that the greatest changes, certainly over the last two or three years, have come about through the music and the physique of the gymnast.

Rhythmic gymnastics has become known as 'the beautiful and elegant sport', with the gymnasts themselves being looked upon as mature, both in physique and in performance. Although there is evidence that the thinner, younger gymnast is becoming more highly regarded, I would sincerely hope that whilst it is essential to encourage youngsters to participate at their own level, the sport will continue to keep its more mature performers until they are well into their twenties and even thirties, as it does now.

Probably the biggest change has occurred in the music. The switch from the compulsory single instrument to the full orchestra for the group performance has added a new dimension to the choreography. There was an initial concern, on my part at least, and which was borne out in the first competition in which music was permitted, that it could become merely background noise. However, I believe that coaches are now beginning to apply themselves to show better use of the various dynamics and instruments used in an orchestral piece.

Though the 'single instrument' rule still applies to the individual competition (i.e. it is compulsory), a number of countries and competitors have sought to move away from the previous tie to the piano and have looked to using other instruments – the guitar, violin, saxophone and drum being the most popular, with others such as harmonica, harpsichord and piano accordion all being tried. In some cases, it has been difficult to decide whether in fact the recording was of just one instrument or more than

Fig 7   A pose showing both maturity and elegance.

So far as the work is concerned, apparatus throws are now twice as high as they were ten years ago, so allowing a greater number and more complex movement elements to be performed underneath. This has only been possible in Great Britain since the era of the high-ceilinged sports hall (which has now become an established part of most towns, and indeed of many schools).

It hardly seems possible now that when I started in rhythmic gymnastics we even had difficulty in obtaining the apparatus to use, and those available often did not conform to the very strict regulations of dimension and weight. This caused many problems, and we went abroad armed with various tools and gadgets for adapting the size of the apparatus. At most international events, the apparatus is checked and marked before the performance – and sometimes after it.

one, so creating problems for judges and organisers. For me, the piano still holds the 'number-one' spot because of its wide-ranging and melodic attributes, but I do feel that the full potential of other instruments has not yet been exploited.

Most of our original equipment was imported, or even hand-made. We still make our own ribbons and sticks, and these are now considered to be superior to many which we

Fig 8   Eye contact projects the personality and gives an air of confidence.

stretch leotard has long since been replaced by a multitude of 'silky' outfits – a sign of the new popular and readily available leisure-wear.

Lastly, the influence of the stage should be mentioned. The highest scoring gymnasts in the world have the 'show business' air about them. They put on a performance for both judges and audience, projecting themselves with supreme confidence, and conveying a truly expressive and dramatic aura which at times leaves the spectators quite breathless.

2 Fundamentals

What are the fundamentals of rhythmic gymnastics? If the lay person was asked this question, I am sure we would be given an answer such as 'Oh, ribbons and hoops and balls and so on.' In fact, this rather vague definition often has to be used to identify rhythmic gymnastics. To so many people, gymnastics spells artistic gymnastics: they think of the vault, the beam and the bars. It would seem that each form is characterised by its apparatus — the artistic gymnasts perform *on* their large fixed apparatus, whilst the rhythmic gymnasts perform *with* their small hand apparatus. Interestingly, it is the apparatus which comes to mind, but what is important in rhythmic gymnastics is not only what is done with the apparatus, but what the body does *together* with the apparatus. Throwing and catching the apparatus is a very risky procedure, made more difficult by the gymnast turning, leaping or rolling whilst the apparatus is in the air, but the body elements and the apparatus elements are of equal importance in rhythmic gymnastics, and we will look at the technique of some of the fundamental skills in this chapter.

THE FACILITY

Before we consider these skills, it is necessary to look at the facility required in order to practise rhythmic gymnastics. Contrary to popular belief, you do not need a gymnasium; in fact it is better if you have not got this facility. Far too much time is spent recovering ropes and ribbons from the girders in the ceiling (this is a technique in itself, usually achieved by throwing the hoop so that it turns over on its own axis, and wraps around the hanging apparatus to pull it down!). It is best to work with a clear overhead space, free of chandeliers, spotlights and rafters: a village or community hall, a school hall, dining hall, theatre, perhaps, or any other 'space' — even the back lawn in summer — but do keep away from the windows, for obvious reasons! Initially it is not necessary to have a really high ceiling, but you will find that as gymnasts grow older, stronger and more advanced, they will throw much higher and eventually outgrow the normal hall.

In addition to the space above, the space below the gymnast is also important. The floor needs to be clean and non-slip, any surface being suitable, although a sprung floor is obviously kinder to the legs and feet. The recognised covering used in top-level work is a carpet, such as the one we have in the lounge at home, but without too much nylon in it, which causes friction burns on the gymnasts' feet and legs. However, a full carpet is an expensive item, large and difficult to store, and so most practice takes place on the bare floor of the hall or gymnasium. Mats may be used, perhaps individually or in strips for practising some of the more difficult elements, but they can sometimes be a hindrance, the rolling hoop getting stuck in the crack between two mats, or the bouncing ball not bouncing because the mat is too spongy!

The size of the full area is 12m × 12m — the same as that for artistic gymnastics, but unless working towards a high-level, senior competition, this is not essential and you can work in whatever space you can find. Much of the body-work, the ballet training, suppleness and strengthening exercises and some of the manipulative skills can be practised at home.

THE DRESS

I suppose participation in any activity involves some financial cost, if only to acquire the right clothing, but this need not be costly for the average performer; a leisure suit, jump suit, or leotard and tights is perfectly adequate – even shorts and a T-shirt. Really, anything which is comfortable without being restricting, and not too baggy, is suitable. Only at competition level does the 'leotard-only' rule apply. Footwear, which is normally an expensive item in sport, is not necessary at all. Many gymnasts work in bare feet, but if you want to be in fashion when on show, you wear the rhythmic gymnastics 'half-shoe'. Leather ones are purchased from recognised suppliers, though these are costly, or you can knit your own from the 'tootsies' pattern available from the BAGA.

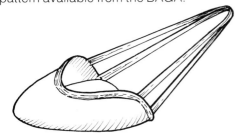

Fig 9   *The rhythmic gymnastics half-shoe.*

THE APPARATUS

Fundamental to the sport of rhythmic gymnastics is the apparatus. It is better if you have your own set, so that you get used to it and can practise with it regularly, especially as it is an advantage if it is matched in size and weight to your physique. Probably the easiest to acquire, and in fact the easiest to start work with, are the rope and the hoop, though the most appealing and the one which everyone wants to try is the ribbon.

The Rope

As long as you ensure it has no handles, this can be acquired at a boatyard, or a climbing and outdoor pursuits department of a sports shop. For most, a 3m length is necessary, preferably a plaited rope, of any synthetic material or hemp, any colour, and about 8mm thick. A small girl will cope with about 2½m in length and 6mm thick. An easy measure is achieved by standing on the centre of the rope and holding the ends which should reach approximately armpit level. If the rope is too long, or for ease of manipulation, a knot may be tied at each end.

The Hoop

The hoop can be bought from a local toy shop. Initially a cheap plastic one is all that is required, of a size reaching approximately hip level when the hoop is stood on the floor at the side of the gymnast. To give added strength, particularly around the seam, or to give extra weight or just a change of colour, many of the gymnasts bind the hoop with coloured tape.

The Ribbon and Stick

The ribbon and stick are best discussed as two separate items, for both are certainly better protected, more easily carried and easier to use if they are detachable from each other. Both also can be made at home,

Fundamentals

Fig 10   *Small white stripes are added to the full binding on the hoop to give variation and strength.*

though the biggest difficulty found will be in obtaining the ribbon. I say this because most materials on the market today are very lightweight and not suitable. They get knotted and tangled easily and often fray at the edges. It is best to use a satin, heavy nylon or silk material. The weight is particularly important in order to be able to work the ribbon and so produce the right shapes with it, and equally to allow it to fly efficiently through the air in the throwing elements.

The ribbon needs to be between 4cm and 6cm in width, but the length will vary according to the size and ability of the gymnast. Only the advanced and senior gymnast should be working with the full 6m length. It is recommended that beginners start with a 4½m ribbon, and young children use a ribbon perhaps as short as 3m.

Fig 11   *Ribbon and stick, though attached for working, can be separated.*

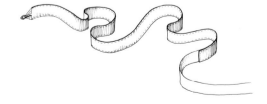

Fig 12   *Double thickness material at the top end of the ribbon.*

If you are going to make your own ribbon, buy more than the required length, so that the first part of the ribbon, near to the stick, can be double thickness. This assists the work of the ribbon by giving extra weight near the attachment. However, because it can be difficult to obtain the correct satin ribbon, generally it is recommended that you buy the stick and ribbon, although if finances are really restricted, consider making just the stick. Though the pukka sticks used by top gymnasts are usually made of plastic or fibreglass, any DIY expert (or novice) could manage to produce a wooden stick at about one tenth of the price of a fibreglass stick. A school woodwork department could perhaps be approached to supply them individually or in bulk. Materials needed are quite easily obtained and are inexpensive, the total cost amounting to about 50p per stick.

If you are going to make your own stick, you will require the following materials:

1. Wood dowel (of 7mm diameter), cut to length between 45cm and 55cm (for youngsters and beginners).
2. Curtain hook, such as a screw-in open-ended eyelet used for net curtains.
3. Swivel, such as a fishing-tackle safety-pin swivel.
4. Glue, such as Araldite or similar.

The dowel is usually available in lengths of 6 or 10 feet from your local DIY shop and once you have sawn it to the required length, the ends can be lightly sandpapered to smooth them down and remove any rough edges. The handle end may be covered if desired with plastic or elastoplast tape, or any other suitable covering, but this is not an essential requirement.

The swivel is acquired from a fishing-tackle shop, and it is recommended that the safety-pin type is purchased. Others are available, notably the key-ring type, but they have been found to be problematic since the ribbon catches on the sharp ends.

The ring end of the swivel is slipped on to the curtain hook which has been prised open sufficiently to allow this. The curtain ring is then squeezed very tightly shut, so that the swivel cannot come off. Once this is done, the curtain hook is screwed and glued into the end of the wood dowel. A very strong glue must be used so that the hook will not pull out during use. The amount of stress placed upon the attachment during the work with the ribbon is very great and if the hook is not firmly in place, it will come adrift within minutes. Let the glue set quite thoroughly and the stick will be ready for

Fig 13   Materials for making the ribbon stick.

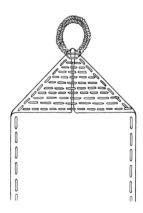

Fig 14   The loop is woven from thread.

use. The ribbon should have a loop at the top end which will slip into the safety-pin attachment on the end of the swivel.

The wooden stick is perfectly adequate for the beginner, and because it is inexpensive, particularly when made in bulk, it is especially suitable for use in schools. The more experienced handyman may try to make a stick from fibreglass, though this will be more expensive, and requires a particular expertise in 'whipping' the swivel attachment on to the end of the fibreglass.

The Ball

Because of its weight the ball is really rather special. It is not until you pick up the rhythmic gymnastics ball that you realise how heavy it is, since it appears to be rather light, like a beach or play ball. Plastic footballs or foam balls can be used initially for practising some of the basics such as rolling and bouncing but these skills are obviously better achieved with the correct type of ball. These can be purchased in two different sizes, a normal full size, and a junior size, suitable for children. Otherwise, the nearest and best matched ball is the volleyball which is quite suitable for practice in school.

Clubs

I would not recommend beginners to acquire clubs at all. Apart from the expense and the fact that there is no real substitute, they are also difficult to work with and are regarded as being more advanced. Because

Fig 15   Clubs exchanges are quite safe for more advanced gymnasts.

of the intricacies of working with two clubs simultaneously, and because the throwing and catching technique, even of small juggling elements, has to be co-ordinated and controlled, they can be quite dangerous. However, some simple swinging moves are beneficial and effective for both general co-ordination practice and as a visual display.

APPARATUS TECHNIQUES

Two particular techniques emerge as being fundamental and common to all pieces of apparatus. These are:

1. Swinging and circling.
2. Throwing and catching.

Fig 17   A difficult but well co-ordinated leap combined with the throw of the ball.

Fig 16   The full circling movement shows clearly with the ribbon.

Swinging and Circling

The technique of 'swing' is based upon a weight transference from one foot to the other and is performed either with the feet apart so that the weight can shift from side to side, or with one foot in front of the other and apart, so that the transference of weight occurs forwards and backwards. The movement must be performed smoothly, with a knee bend, and going through what is termed the *plié* position (the term *plié* comes from the world of ballet).

During this weight transference between the feet, the apparatus is held in one hand and swung either side to side or forwards and backwards, depending on how the feet are split. In the case of the rope and the hoop, care must be taken not to hit the floor with the apparatus. This is ensured by stretching the arm out and away from the body (this same technique also applies to the other apparatus). Because of its length it is not possible to keep the ribbon off the floor, but it is important in all cases that the movement should not be jerky, but rather flowing and continuous.

The swinging movement described can be repeated several times as a practice exercise, and the side swing can be developed to link into a full circling movement of the arm, with a step–together–step (*chassé*) of the feet, or into a turn with a step–step–step of the feet. The forward and backwards swing can be developed into a small throw and catch (toss) of the apparatus, or into a forward or backward travelling step.

It is important to practise this type of swinging movement so that it becomes fluent and easy to perform while holding the apparatus in your hand. In part, it forms the basis of many other movements, particularly the element of throwing and catching which is discussed next.

Throwing and Catching

As stated earlier, throwing is common to each apparatus and is an essential part of the choreography of rhythmic gymnastics. For the gymnast to be able to perform a single, double or even triple forward roll, or leaps, turns or bends etc. whilst the apparatus is in the air, much practice in the art of throwing is necessary, and the mastery of catching the apparatus too!

What is being performed 'under' the apparatus will dictate the speed and the angle of the throw. Knowing also that it is important to show a variety of throws and catches, it is necessary to use different grips and different directions. However, before any of these more complex techniques can be attempted, the basic throw must be mastered.

Because this skill has to be performed with

Fig 18   It is important to follow through with the arm in the throwing action.

the use of one hand only, I would recommend that the beginner starts with the hoop as it is easier to grip and control. Hold the hoop in the right hand in overgrasp and swing the arm down to the side and back, keeping the hoop parallel to the body. As the arm goes back, the wrist will be cocked with the back of the hand facing the floor; the grip should be firm. Next, the arm swings through to stretch forwards and upwards into the throwing action. Try to keep the arm as straight as possible – this will be difficult if it is too close to the body because the hoop will hit the floor. Remember to keep the arm away from the body; you might even lean to the left side a little. As the arm reaches a position above and just in front of the head, at an angle of about 160 degrees to the horizontal, the fingers are opened firmly and the hoop is projected off the index finger into the air. If the hoop is released at this angle it will rise vertically and come back into a comfortable position for catching without you having to move your feet. In this way, you can practise repetition throws until perfect.

The catching procedure is simply a reverse action of the throw. Reach up with an outstretched arm in preparation for the catch, and take the hoop as high and as early as possible in an overgrasp grip. As contact is made, the arm swings down and back at the side of the body together with the hoop so that the whole action is smooth and fluid.

I have suggested that the hoop is the easiest piece of apparatus with which to start practising throws and since each piece varies considerably, each has its own individual characteristics. Because of these different sizes and shapes, and because one apparatus is rigid and another flexible, the technique for throwing and catching varies somewhat from apparatus to apparatus. This will be considered under the respective apparatus chapter headings.

Fig 19   Juggling is one of the more difficult elements.

General Handling Skills

General manipulative skills with the apparatus involve many actions with the hands such as spinning, rolling, rotating, tossing, juggling, bouncing etc, but other parts of the body are also used – particularly the feet, legs, shoulders and back.

Variety is essential, and the use of different directions and different levels can produce very creative movements. You should aim to work with the apparatus in new and unusual ways (as well as around the established characteristics of each piece) and to provide interesting and well-judged exercises.

BODY MOVEMENT ELEMENTS

The sport is built and in the main judged upon the body-work, and as all the techniques and skills of the apparatus are performed with certain specific body movements, it is vital that these body elements are practised and perfected.

Elements of dance steps, jumps and leaps, pivots and turns, balances, body waves and body bends are the listed essentials. They must be performed with control, lightness, elevation, suppleness and full extension as well as elegance and poise.

Whilst there are specific named movements which are recognisable in rhythmic gymnastics (the split leap, the arabesque and the pivot turn, for example) there are endless other movement possibilities within the categories listed, so allowing much freedom for expression and room for originality and invention. The movement combinations possible between body and apparatus are seemingly infinite, and the creation of new and unusual movement patterns is both exciting and challenging for the gymnast and for the coach.

Steps

Beginning with the feet gives you the opportunity to step out or stamp out various rhythms, and these rhythms lead to the formation of a variety of step patterns, which on the one hand may be very intricate, or on the other hand quite simple (and yet equally effective). Of great importance is the actual footwork itself, which must be 'clean' and precise, the steps being very definite in direction and quality. The ankles and feet should be very resilient, much of the work being performed on the toes, particularly the light and springy types of step. Other steps which are perhaps in the Russian or Spanish style are characteristically required to be performed on the flat foot, but must still show the necessary strength and precision.

The importance of ballet training becomes apparent not only for the promotion of leg strength, elegance, and upper-body-work, but particularly for the improvement of footwork. Toes should be pointed, the feet and ankles stretched for the majority of the time, but equally there must be some 'give' in the foot and ankle to provide resilience and bounce.

Many of the steps used are in fact derived from ballet and so the terminology used is

Fig 20   Position of the hands and arms as well as the feet show a truly Spanish style.

Figs 21–24 A series of ballet exercises showing stretching and flexing of the ankle and the knee – this will help to develop good footwork.

Fig 22

Fig 23

Fig 24

18

Fig 25   Strengthening the legs and feet.

the same, i.e. all the names are in French. The following are a few examples of the most commonly used step patterns:

1.   *Chassé.* Step right, close left to right, step right. Repeat and step left, close right to left, step left. This is a basic three-step pattern, sometimes described as step–together–step, and is an important combination as it forms the preparation for many other movements. When performed with forward travel at some speed it is used as a lead-in to leaps, particularly the split leap. If you take off from the right foot, and leap from right leg to left, the *chassé* is begun with the right foot, so that the last step of the *chassé* becomes the take-off step for the leap. Try the *chassé* followed by: a hop on one foot; a tuck jump taking off from one foot; a komat jump (*see* page 20).

2.   Polka. Precede the *chassé* step with a hop on one foot and you have the polka.

This is a livelier, springier step and like the *chassé* step, it can be developed and made interesting by being performed in different directions, or with a turn, or as a preparation for some travelling steps or leaps.

3.   *Jeté.* Small or large springing movements from one foot to the other are termed *jetés. Petits jetés* (small springs) are usually performed with the feet and knees turned out; *grands jetés* (large springs) require greater elevation and become more like the leap from one foot to the other.

4.   Stutter. Currently a very popular step, often used to highlight a particularly fast or 'rumbly' phrase of music – the feet patter very rapidly indeed, either on the spot or travelling a short distance in any direction. It is a very effective movement if choreographed to the right piece of music, and though it would appear to be a simple step, at speed it is difficult to perform well.

Fundamentals

Many other steps of British and international origin, of various dance styles and characterisations are used, all of which should, of course, be interpretive of the music which is being worked to. Each individual gymnast will have their own style of performance and will feel at ease with certain types of music, and so the selection of music to suit the gymnast's personality, age and level of work is a particularly important factor.

Leaps and Jumps

The technique of jumping demands much effort in training if good elevation and a fully extended body shape are to be achieved. However, before launching into the practice of take-offs, it is vital that the landing technique is worked upon. So many gymnasts land heavily and so risk damage to their knees, feet and even their spine that the coach must ensure before all else that the gymnast can land safely and well without jarring either legs or back. The landing should be very resilient, toes touching the floor first, and then the rest of the foot; the ankle, knee and hip giving into the floor to cushion the landing. The following are some exercises for practising landing:

1. Take small jumps on the spot, feet together, stretching the feet and pointing the toes in the air, and bending the knees on landing. (These small jumps when performed with the feet turned out slightly are called *sautés*.)
2. Jump from both feet from a low height. (bench or box top), to land on the floor, feet together, landing with control and resilience.
3. Run and spring from one foot, landing on two feet with resilience.
4. Run and leap, taking off from one foot

and landing on the other with lightness and resilience.

Once some of the above practices have been worked upon to improve the landings, more attention can be paid to the take-off, which should be forceful and dynamic. The knee and ankle should bend on the take-off, and there should be a strong drive through the leg which extends to push the body into the air. Strength in the legs is fundamental to a good leaping action; the body must be equally strong, and held with tension in whatever shape is chosen according to the style of leap performed. There is a danger that in attempting to elevate the body and maintain this strong position in the air the gymnast will also lift her shoulders and create a very tight and hunched position in the upper body. This is difficult to correct and a determined effort to press the shoulders down must be worked upon.

The name given to a leap or jump is normally indicative of the shape which the body adopts whilst in the air, and it is therefore necessary to be precise with the position not only of the body, but also of the arms and legs. Some of the jumps and leaps which are commonly used and which form a fundamental part of the sequence are:

1. Tuck jump. Take off from one or two feet, bring both knees up high in front of the chest and land on two feet.
2. Komat jump. Similar to the tuck jump with knees up in front, but take-off must be from one foot only, and the knees come up one after the other. Legs 'change' in the air, so the landing is on the other foot.
3. Split leap. Leap forwards from one foot to the other, legs splitting wide, and reaching a horizontal position in the air, one forwards and one backwards.
4. Stag leap. Similar to split leap, but front

Fig 26 Tuck jump with good elevation and expression.

Fig 27 The second knee should come really high before straightening out.

Fig 28　Keep the legs straight and wide in the split leap.

Fig 29　The side leap requires both flexibility and strength.

leg is bent under, back leg remains straight. Take-off and landing can be from one or two feet.

5. Side leap. The difficulty of getting both legs up to the horizontal position becomes very apparent in the side leap. From a forward take-off, the body makes a sharp quarter-turn and then the gymnast must consciously work to lift both legs at the same time, forcing them up in an obliquely forward position rather than a sideways position (as the name implies).

As with all body movements, there is an infinite number of variations. This is evident with the leaps and jumps where both the take-offs and landings can be performed using one or two feet, and the body positions can be either tucked or wide or a combination of both.

Fig 30　Prepare well for the pivot turn.

Turns

The recognised pivot turn requires tension and leg strength (as with the leaps) plus good balance. It is essential that the body stays upright with the weight over the supporting leg, otherwise the gymnast will not maintain balance throughout the full one or two turns. The turn should be performed high on the toes, and practice of the *relevé* (rising up on to the toes) on one foot will not only help the balance position, but will improve the leg strength too, particularly if it is repeated ten or twenty times.

Pivot Turn

Start in a small lunge position with your weight over your front (left) leg, which is slightly bent, and with your back leg straight, feet flat on the floor, your right arm sideways and your left arm forwards, both at shoulder height. Pull the weight sharply forwards and

Fig 31　Pull up high on the toes during the turn.

Fig 32 Keep the free leg high on exit from the turn.

upwards whilst rising up on to the toes of your front foot, at the same time opening the front arm out to the side and swinging your straight back leg in a circular movement round to the front, then bending your knee to bring the foot in to touch the other knee. The turn has now been initiated and should be smooth but strong. Once the action has been started, both arms go up above the head into the fifth position (both arms overhead in a curved position, palms facing each other).

Current regulations within the *Code of Points* demand that pivot turns be specifically included in the ribbon exercise. Though all body elements must be present in all exercises, there is a special requirement for the ribbon of at least three different types of pivot turn. From the basic technique described above, variation by way of turning towards the supporting leg, or away from the supporting leg can be practised, or, by increasing the amount of turn, you can change it into a double or even triple, or simply alter the position of the free leg. The attitude turn is very effective and is achieved by lifting the back leg up and into a bent

Fig 33 Attitude balance.

position, with the leg turned out at the hip (as for the attitude in ballet).

Adding other simpler turns improves the general impression of a routine, and these could include turning on other parts of the body such as the bottom, knees or back. A basic patter turn involving little steps turning on the spot becomes more effective when the apparatus work is more intricate, such as a coiling action with the ribbon or a rotation overhead with the hoop.

Balances

The technique of balance is similar to that of the pivot turn, for the important factor here is stability. To achieve this, the whole weight of the body must be directly above the point of balance or base, which is most usually the foot.

The body must also show tension – any movement, particularly of the limbs, or any slight relaxing of the muscles will cause a wobble and so pull the body off balance. The body line must be exact, and the body shape held, without the shoulders hunching up.

Fig 34   Extension is necessary in all balances.

Attitude Balance

This position is as described in the pivot turn above. The attitude is a ballet position, and is effective when held with the weight still over one foot.

Arabesque Balance

Another ballet position, this time with the leg extended high behind. The higher the leg will go, the lower the shoulders are permitted to drop. However, do not allow the line of the back to break, i.e. do not let the leg stay low and the shoulders drop down as this creates a poor line of the body.

Balances on other parts of the body, though interesting and seemingly easy, become more difficult when the apparatus skill is added, for it is difficult to maintain the motion of the apparatus during low-level balance. Equally, balances on a flat foot are relatively easy, and so do not carry the same difficulty value as balances on the toes of one foot (which if held for two seconds are of superior difficulty). In any case, though seeking to maintain a position of stability and perfect stillness with the body, the

Fig 35   Practise balance without apparatus.

apparatus must be kept in motion or must be used to effect the balance itself, thus adding greatly to the difficulty of the combined skill.

Body Waves

To be able to isolate movement of various parts of the body requires a certain degree of flexibility; training in the correct technique is also required, and above all else a great deal of concentration on the job in hand.

The body wave is such a fluid movement that a complete and true 'ripple' through the entire body is extremely difficult. Many gymnasts wave their arms around in the pretence of doing a body wave, but so often the

Fig 36   *Difficulty is increased with the use of apparatus.*

body itself is doing very little. For this reason, I suggest that the learning stages should deal solely with the movement of the spine, with the arms eventually following the movement rather than initiating it. There are a number of practices which will help achieve the right sort of feeling for the body wave:

1.   Stand with the feet a little way apart, and with the arms out sideways; try to flatten the back, keeping the head in line with the body. You might need someone to correct your position or stand sideways-on to a mirror, turning your head to see if you have achieved a completely flat back position.
2.   From the position described above, lift the shoulders and round the top part of the spine, pulling the stomach in and pressing the shoulder blades upwards.
3.   Relax the knees and arms, and try to round the whole of the back to obtain a curled position through the spine.
4.   From a kneeling position on the floor, sit back on the heels and curl forwards over the knees. Gradually arch up lifting the top part of the back first, then push the hips forward and arch back leaving the head till last.
5.   Lie on your back on the floor, with arms stretched out sideways. Arch up to sitting, pushing the chest upwards first, and leaving the head and shoulders till last, then bend forwards curling the back over the legs. Lie down by sinking back and uncurling slowly, head touching the floor last.
6.   Finally, try the full body wave in a standing position, first facing and holding a bar or ledge about waist height, and pushing through from the ankles, knees and then hips. Then turn sideways and practise the body wave using one arm which goes in the opposite direction to the ripple of the body.

An additional useful practice which you

Fig 37 Aim to get the back absolutely flat.

Fig 38 Isolate the hunch to the upper body.

Fig 39   Curve the whole spine.

Fig 40   From a kneeling position, the body wave can be achieved solely
through the spine.

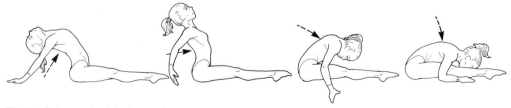

Fig 41   Get a good arch before curling.

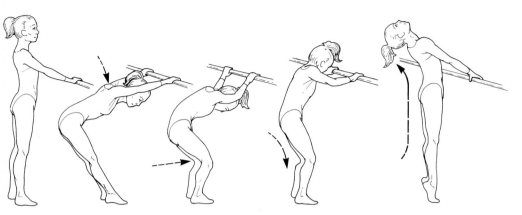

Fig 42   Start the wave from the feet.

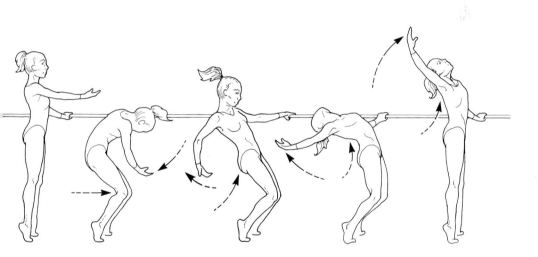

Fig 43   Allow the arm to follow rather than initiate the movement.

could use in the gymnasium if you have access to climbing ropes is the following:

Sit down on the floor between two ropes, and stretching up with your arms, hold one rope in each hand. Bend your knees up to place your feet flat on the floor about a foot away from your bottom. Using your arms to pull, push your feet, knees, and hips forward to stand, leaving the chest and head till last.

Much practice of this type of movement is necessary if any result is to be noticeable, and it would be difficult to progress to more challenging variations (such as performing the body wave on one foot, or performing the side body wave or the reverse body wave) until the gymnast has the ability and control over the various segments of the spine needed for the basic body wave.

Fundamentals

Bends

The gymnast who has a very flexible spine and who is able to bend easily will have no trouble in performing the back-bend, whereas the stiffer gymnast will be restricted in her movement and will become frustrated because of her physical inability to reach a back-bend position. However, a word of warning should be issued to gymnasts both to prepare themselves thoroughly *before* attempting the extreme bend, and to learn the technique correctly. Injuries can be caused not just from over-stretching or from dropping backwards too quickly, but from a poor recovery, usually caused by a lack of strength in the mid-body region. It is vital that the gymnast is taught to 'pull up' after the bend to return to a good standing posture; this, of course, will be aided by some strength work with the abdominal muscles.

The back-bend is best learned first in a kneeling position (as is the side-bend) since the hand can be used for support.

Back-Bend

Kneel on one knee, with your front leg extended forwards on the floor. Place one hand behind on the floor or the leg, and then bend backwards as far as is comfortable, stretching the free arm overhead. Recover by pulling up to a straight body position, still kneeling, with tummy in, back straight and both arms above the head.

Fig 44   First stage of a back-bend.

Fig 45 Keep the hips directly over the supporting leg.

Side-Bend

Kneel on one knee, with your leg extended sideways on the floor. Place one hand on the floor at the side of the bent leg, and bend sideways away from the straight leg, your top arm reaching overhead. Recover to the straight body position on one knee. Next practise the side-bend in a standing position on one foot. Reach upwards with the arm before bending sideways, so that a good line is achieved, and your hip does not stick out.

Fig 46 Maintain a good body line and tension.

Fig 47   It is important to practise the back-bend on the other side too.

Similarly, when ready to progress to learning the back-bend in a standing position, keep the weight firmly planted over one foot and begin the extension into the bend from the very top of the spine. Do not let the hips drop forwards or the knee bend too much. Your arms should start above the head and the head and eyes should follow the hand or hands back overhead.

The clubs serve a useful purpose here in the practice of the back-bend movement for they act as an extension of the arm. With a club in each hand and weight on one foot, stretch both arms overhead and lean backwards to touch the floor with the tips of both clubs. Recover by standing up straight, reaching upwards with your arms beside your ears.

Acrobatics

In addition to the body elements described above, certain acrobatic type moves are allowed, but on a very restricted basis in comparison to the floorwork tumbles of artistic gymnastics. For instance, elements of the handstand and cartwheel variety are not permitted, nor are those of the handspring or somersault type. However, certain very basic gymnastics elements are allowed, and it is simpler to list what is actually permitted rather than what is not; these are called pre-acrobatic elements:

1.   Forward or backward roll performed without flight (i.e. not a dive forward roll).
2.   Splits, when performed as a fluid movement and without an obvious stop in the splits position.
3.   Supporting weight on the hand or hands but again without stopping, and without the body reaching a vertical position, as in a handstand.
4.   Support on the chest or shoulders without stopping in this position.

From the above list, it is apparent that there is little room for the agility of gymnastics, especially as there is an additional rule stating that no more than three of these pre-acrobatic elements are allowed in any one routine. You will perhaps notice that the sideways roll is not included in this list, because it is not counted as an acrobatic element at all. Gymnasts have pounced upon this 'loophole' and used it to provide difficulty and excitement within their routine. As there is no limit to the number of side rolls performed, we now see as many as three consecutive rolls whilst the apparatus is in the air. Of course they must be performed at speed, and because of this have lost their true 'sideways' direction. The roll has become a unique form of half sideways and half forward roll, and is known as the 'scrabble roll' – scrabble for short.

Whilst concentrating on these acrobatic type elements, it is important not to forget about the apparatus and what it is doing. The triple scrabble commented on above is performed during a throwing element and is of course difficult to do. It is necessary to start with one roll first and practise this together with the throwing and catching. Other apparatus elements can also be performed during these acrobatic feats but at all times the apparatus must be kept moving. It should not be held in a static position, nor should it be left in a static position on the floor. The important factor is continuity of movement, and this applies to both body and apparatus.

MUSICAL ACCOMPANIMENT

The essence of rhythmic gymnastics is the ability to harmonise body and apparatus work, which in turn interprets and expresses the rhythm and quality of the accompanying music.

Having discussed briefly the fundamentals of the apparatus techniques and body elements we turn now to the aspect of music – a very important part of rhythmic gymnastics. All the exercises are performed to music and all the work in performance should be a direct reflection of the music, be it classical, jazz, rock 'n roll or whatever.

It is not imperative to be a musician to be a rhythmic gymnast or coach, but it most certainly helps if you have a sense of rhythm and you appreciate and understand music, if only a little. Simply to know the difference between beats, and be able to count or tap out a basic 2/4 or 3/4 rhythm helps (i.e. to recognise whether there are *two* beats or *three* beats in the bar). This is important in understanding and 'feeling' the type of movement which suits the two or three-beat type of music, because they are very different.

Three-beat music is essentially a waltz time, and whether played quickly or slowly it suggests a lilting or swaying movement, whereas the two-beat music is more pulsating and suggests a sharper movement, that of marching or springing. This is a very basic description and of course there are other more complex time signatures which in the initial stages we need not concern ourselves with. Most of us know what type of music we like listening to – why not ask yourself whether you could move to it? If you have a feeling for the melody or the beat, you might find yourself tapping your foot, or your fingers, or nodding and swaying your head in time with it. You might even feel the urge to get up and dance to it. However, I would suggest that it is only the overall rhythm which you are affected by, and that there are other more meaningful factors which become apparent if you listen carefully and try to analyse the music. By this I mean, for example, the contrasting qualities of strong and light, achieved by using the full range of notes on the instrument: the low (bass) notes giving the impression of heaviness; the higher (treble) notes giving an impression of lightness; the use of many notes up and down the keyboard (arpeggios), perhaps in quick succession, giving a feeling of broadness and power, or the

Fundamentals

playing of a single note giving a softer and lighter impression.

Tempo

Speed (tempo) is also a major factor for consideration, and not simply whether the music is slow or fast. Do you think that slow music played 'in the bass' creates a different impression to slow music played 'in the treble'? Similarly, compare fast music played in the bass with that played in the treble. You will probably find that they do sound very different, and so are open to different interpretations in terms of movement.

Many other combinations of tempo, quality and rhythm are possible – particularly on the piano keyboard. Because of its vast range and the use of two hands in playing, it is possible not only to create a great variety of sounds, but also to vary the sounds within one piece of music. For instance, the right and left hands could be playing differently, thus giving two options for interpretation – it could even be that the body expresses one option, and the apparatus the other!

The orchestra is obviously able to offer a wide variation of sound with its large number of instruments but it is only recently that full orchestral accompaniment has been allowed, and this applies solely to the group exercises. Individuals must still perform to music played on one instrument by one instrumentalist. In some ways, particularly in the search for suitable music, this is limiting. Recently there has been a trend in 'other instrument' music, that is music played on instruments other than the piano, such as the guitar, violin, saxophone, drum, xylophone or harpsichord. This has created some variation, particularly for the ear, but in many cases the music has lacked melody and contrast and has become merely a backround noise to the movement.

Unless you have your own drummer or guitarist for example, you may have problems finding suitable music, and are left with cutting and splicing music from record or tape, or finding a pianist who will play some short pieces for you to record. Alternatively, you can acquire music already prepared and recorded to the correct length, especially for rhythmic gymnastics. There are a number of these tapes available containing a variety of different types of music suitable for gymnasts of differing ages.

Choice of music

Here are some points to bear in mind when selecting music for your own exercises:

1. Make sure the music is not too long. The rules state that each individual exercise should be between sixty and ninety seconds in length; usually seventy-five seconds is quite sufficient. For beginners or young gymnasts it is even better to have it shorter than this, perhaps sixty-five or seventy seconds. You should most definitely avoid having music which is too near the maximum or minimum length – playing speeds and timekeepers can vary!
2. Select music which suits your age and ability – not too strong and broad, nor too slow, which requires large movements performed with full extension and suits the more mature gymnast.
3. Choose something which has a contrast of both tempo and rhythm. You cannot move at the same speed or in the same way throughout the whole exercise, and indeed it would become boring, unless you have the experience to carry it off.
4. Identify music which contains elements that bring out the main characteristics of the apparatus, i.e. some two-beat fairly fast music for skipping with the rope, some short

rhythmic patterns to highlight the bouncing of the ball, or a slower, stronger phrase for swinging and circling the hoop.

5. Finally, consider the type of music you want to work to: classical, jazz, pop, modern, rock 'n roll, boogie, Latin American, folk, or whatever.

All styles are acceptable. Some are more difficult to work to than others and suit some people and not others. So choose what you feel is right for you and what you feel you can express; then begin choreographing your sequence.

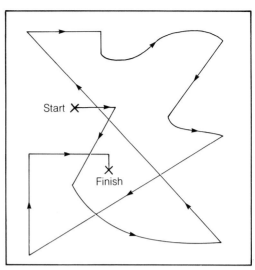

Fig 48   Floor plan.

SEQUENCES

From the emphasis placed in this chapter on the continuity of movement, it is obvious that sequence work plays an important part in rhythmic gymnastics, and from the outset it is of value when practising to link two or three movements together. There are occasions when some elements need to be mastered and practised in isolation, but they will not become part of the whole sequence unless they link in fluently and easily with the movements which precede and follow. A full sequence will, through training, become a series of short phrases and can be practised as such. However, there is a danger here of the sequence becoming disjointed and lacking in fluency because either the breaks between phrases have always been marked in the same place, or the routine has not been performed sufficiently often in its entirety.

Composition

In constructing the sequence there are a number of considerations which are important for good composition. You must bear in mind that of the ten marks awarded for an individual voluntary exercise (as judged by the international *Code of Points* book), seven marks are given for composition. This is a large proportion of the total and although you might in some competitions be judged upon a junior code or a special schools code, you will still find that the majority of points are given for composition. The other marks are awarded for the execution or performance of the routine.

The following are some of the points which you should consider when constructing the exercise:

1. Try to cover all the floor area; the corners, the sides and the middle of the square should be used at least once. You should sometimes move in a clockwise direction, sometimes anticlockwise; sometimes work in straight lines and sometimes in a curve. In order to achieve all this, you must include quite a number of travelling movements, so avoid putting in too much static work. Also, to create a better impression, do not start or finish your sequence too near the outside edge of the area. To help you

Fig 49   Creating new movements in pairs.

visualise the floor patterns, and to make sure that you are including a variety of pathways and directions it will help if you draw out a floor plan.

2.   Make sure you include a variety of the difficult elements; you should therefore perform all the body movement skills – step, jump, turn, balance, wave and bend. Some may be repeated, particularly if there is one movement which you are good at, but avoid over-use of any one type, especially if this is to the exclusion of another.

3.   Space out the difficult elements through the exercise, avoid having too many of one type close together, and do not leave them all till the end when you may be getting tired and perhaps lose concentration.

4.   Link the skills together in a logical fashion and try to find the direction of movement which is natural or easy for you to adopt after your previous move. Some changes of direction of the apparatus can be achieved by turning the body, by taking a step with the feet or perhaps by momentarily checking the movement of the apparatus before continuing in another direction.

5.   Create and use some new elements or linking moves. Play around in practice with different ways of throwing and catching the apparatus, try different ways of rolling or twisting on the floor, use different parts of the body to balance on or for manipulating the apparatus. Sometimes, too, you will find a new move by making a mistake in practising or working something out. Be ready for this, and try to remember what it was you did, so that you can repeat it.

The above points count for a small part of the overall composition, but they are factors which lend themselves to an interesting and varied exercise which will be given immediate credit by judges.

Having digested the information given previously in the chapter about the musical accompaniment, you should be in a position to earn up to one mark, which is given for 'the relationship between the music and the movement', International Gymnastics Federation, *Code of Points* (RSG Committee 1982), page 22. Interpreting the quality of the music, working out the movements which best fit the varying speeds of the music and picking out the strong rhythmic patterns with the feet or with the apparatus will all count towards this vital part.

Finally, the largest chunk of the compositional marks goes to the value of the difficult elements. The number and degree of the difficulties will depend upon the level of the competition entered. In schools competitions, the inclusion of all body elements must be apparent and well performed, but at this level the inclusion of the highly superior elements are not required.

Group Work

It would seem appropriate at this stage to mention group work – a choreography usually for six gymnasts who all work together in a sequence which demonstrates the individual elements of body and apparatus work, and also requires that the gymnasts exchange apparatus with each other by passing, throwing, rolling, or any other method of releasing and receiving. Based upon partner and trio-work which build up to the full group exercise, it can be extremely challenging and exciting, and many gymnasts prefer the security of working with others, and of creating new movements and exchanges with each other.

Fig 50   Warming up with the rope.

The limitation of six performers applies in competition only, and so for display purposes you may have as many gymnasts on stage at any one time as you desire. Popular items for display (and now in competition, too) are the duet and the trio.

BODY PREPARATION

I have left until last in this chapter the subject of preparation and conditioning. Fundamental to participation in any sport is proper training and if you intend to take the sport of rhythmic gymnastics really seriously, then of course you must train adequately, prepare your body for the practice you are going to undertake and involve yourself in a specific programme of fitness training. The more suppleness, stamina and strength that you have, as well as co-ordination and control, the more success you will have.

Preparation starts with the warm-up. Do not attempt to undertake any activity without first doing a little stretching of the toes, ankles and calf muscles before getting really warm with some jogging or jumping, or using your rope for some skipping. This is ideal practice since you have the rope anyway and even boxers skip for their warm-up and for stamina training. Alternatively, this could be an opportunity to practise some of the faster or springier dance steps, and get warm at the same time. After that you should move on to some general stretching of other parts of the body such as the trunk, the shoulders and hips, the hamstring muscles (back of the thigh), the wrists and fingers, and of course the spine.

This could be followed by some ballet exercises, which are now regarded as a vital part of the rhythmic gymnast's training. Simple foot stretching, knee bending, leg lifting and holding, rising on to the toes, and use of the arms and head not only assist in strengthening and training the correct movement techniques, but also serve to promote a graceful and elegant line.

More specific mobility work and strength exercises are also essential, and ideas for these are given in Chapter 8.

3 Rope

SKIPPING

The fundamental movement with the rope must surely be skipping. Many other manipulations are also possible and gymnasts tend at times to get carried away with the various intricate skills of one-end releases, lassos, wraps, checks, swings, throws etc. However, since there are strict stipulations about the inclusion of skipping in the exercise, it is vital to ensure that sufficient is included – and seen to be included. Competition judges are looking specifically for the major characteristic of each of the pieces of the apparatus, and penalties occur if they are not present.

Two particular rules, concerned with passing through the rope, refer to the normal skipping action of hops and skips, and to the larger skipping action involving leaps or jumps.

1. Skips and hops. The exercise must contain three different series of skips or hops into the rope, two of which must be done whilst travelling. (A series normally contains a minimum of three skips or steps.)
2. Jumps and leaps. One series of a minimum of three successive jumps or leaps into the rope is required (in addition to the skips and hops mentioned above).

The clever coach or gymnast will ensure that there are more than the required number of elements present in the sequence as choreographed. Should there be a mistake in performance, a trip over the rope, a drop of the rope or some other fumble resulting in the full amount of skips or jumps not being shown, then deductions will be made. By including extra elements, there is less risk of penalties being made for omission.

An additional ruling concerning the skips and jumps states that the rope must be handled in a variety of ways when these moves are being performed. For instance, the rope should perhaps be turned in different directions, not just forwards but backwards and sideways too, and with the arms in different positions such as open or crossed and so on. There is room here for you to create a variety of combinations using the skipping action, perhaps also involving changes of speed of the rope turn. The following are some suggestions.

Types of Skipping

Half-Time Skips

These are also called rebound skips; the rope turns slowly, with two jumps to each turn of the rope. Start with the feet together, and turning the rope forwards, jump over it as it turns, then immediately rebound with another little jump. Count one–two, one–two, one–two, one–two (two counts for each rope turn).

The same rope turn and rhythm can be used for the jogging skips. Instead of jumping with the feet together, jog on the spot and spring over the rope on every alternate step, so that the same foot jumps over the rope each time. You can still count one–two, one–two, one–two, one–two, or skip-step, skip-step, skip-step, skip-step.

Other variations in step patterns may be used, such as a spring and hop, with the free leg bending up in front or behind, or stretching out in front or behind. Scottish-dancing experts might be able to introduce some of the Highland Fling steps – perhaps the *pas de bas* which is a quick one–two–three springing step, or you might find some variations of your own to include.

Single-Time Skips

The common name for these is boxer skips, since they are similar to the skipping action used by the boxing fraternity as part of their stamina training. It involves a faster turn of the rope (try forwards first), and one skip step over the rope with each turn. The feet are really jogging again, the same as in the half-time skips, the difference being just in the turn of the rope. The action feels different because the movement becomes more even with each foot jumping over the rope. The counting is continuous: one, two, three, four, five, six, seven, eight. Try seeing how many skips you can do without tripping over the rope. Can you manage to do twenty? If so, aim for fifty or a hundred. As mentioned earlier, this is a good activity for warming-up and for building up stamina.

Try to keep the arms fairly straight and low, only slightly lifted away from the sides, and use the wrists to initiate the rope turn. At all costs, you should avoid too much elbow action and also ensure that your feet stay low.

You might find it easier to do these skips with the feet together, so that you are jumping from two feet on to two feet each time over the rope – or alternatively, try a hopping action, doing eight hops on the right foot, and eight hops on the left foot.

Double Skips

As the name implies, the double skip involves the rope turning twice for one jump over it. This used to be called 'bumps' many moons ago (before rhythmic gymnastics was invented!). The rope must obviously turn very fast, mostly with a wrist action rather than arm action, so keep the arms low again, and ensure that the feet stay low. Initially, the double skip is best learned by beginning with a few single-time skips, performed with the feet together. Get a good rhythm going first, then attempt one double skip with the quick turn of the rope. It will take a little practice and co-ordination but once you have achieved one, you can begin to practise them in succession, and see how many you can do. If you can manage four without stopping, then you have a superior element to put into your routine.

From these basic skipping actions, you can begin to develop variation by:

1. Changing the step pattern with the feet.
2. Turning the rope backwards instead of forwards.
3. Crossing the arms on some skips.
4. Travelling along whilst skipping.
5. Turning the rope sideways.

The last suggestion is not to be confused with skipping sideways, in which you turn the rope forwards whilst moving in a sideways direction, usually with a gallop-step, bringing the feet together in the air when jumping over the rope.

For the rope turning sideways, stretch one arm forwards, and the other backwards so that the rope is swung across the body from side to side using a wrist action. This is most easily performed with the feet together.

Fig 51   Forward skipping with arms crossed.

Fig 52   Split leap through the rope.

Fig 53   Variation on a stag leap.

Jumps and Leaps

Jumps and leaps are simply an extension of the skipping action – in fact exactly that. The movement becomes larger and usually travels more, and the technique of the rope turning becomes a shoulder action rather than a wrist action.

You can begin to learn these from the simple half-time jogging skip. Begin on the spot, then start to travel with the skip–step, skip–step, and gradually extend the skip over the rope into a bigger leap. You must push from the take-off foot and stretch the front leg forwards in order to get more height and get a stretched position with the legs. If you are supple, and can get the legs wide, you will be able to show the splits position in the air, thus performing what is called the split leap. You should feel the arms making a really big circle, stretching high overhead and then swinging down at the side of the body during the leap.

Once the technique of the split leap is learned, a second leap could be added so two are performed in succession (if landing from the leap on the left foot, take a step and immediately push off from the right foot into the second leap – the leap comes on the same leg every time). Alternatively, the front leg can be bent up and then straightened during the leap to form the stag leap.

Try a tuck jump too, taking off from one or both feet, and bringing the knees up high to the chest. This is a jump which could be performed either on the spot or travelling, and could also be performed with a double turn of the rope as well as a single turn.

At all times during skipping, the rope should be held lightly in the fingers, using a normal grip between the thumb and forefinger to allow for easy manipulation. The arms should be stretched, though not rigid, and should be away from the body. Try always to keep the rope in a smooth curve – it should not kink or hit the floor.

The footwork should be light and springy, with the ankles stretched and toes pointed towards the floor, and the knees and ankles bending on take-off as well as on landing.

Skipping Combinations

Having mastered some of these skips, the next stage is to put together a combination using different step patterns, different speeds with the rope, and changes from forward to backward skipping, and vice versa.

This change of direction of the rope swing can be achieved simply by pausing momentarily with the feet together and allowing the rope to swing forwards and down at the side of the body, then reversing it into the backward skip. Similarly, at the end of the backward skip, just allow the rope to sway forwards by reaching forwards with the arms, then swing it back under the feet to begin the forward skip.

SWINGS

We come quite naturally now to the swings with the rope. These are basic movements needed as links and preparations for individual elements. It is important to learn these alongside the skipping elements, for they help to improve the general handling technique with the rope. Because it is a flexible piece of apparatus, the rope is difficult to control, especially in some of the very simple moves which require co-ordination and extension. With the swinging movements in particular – unless the arms and the whole body extend fully at the end of the swing – the rope will flick up and it will be difficult to maintain the shape for the return swing.

Types of Swing

There are two types of rope swing: the open rope swing and the folded rope swing. Because it is a natural progression from the forward and backward skipping exercises, and because the rope is held ready in two hands, the open rope swing is probably best learned first, using the same 'plane' as the skipping movement.

Planes

A plane, in terms of movement, is described as an area of space around the body through which we can swing the apparatus, or indeed move the body. It is a directional term used in relation to the body itself, and helps to identify the various pathways of movement (there are three) of both the body and the apparatus. It is important that these planes are understood and used, so that the movement of the apparatus is clear and precise, and definite changes from one plane to another are apparent. The three are:

1. The sagittal ('wheel') plane. The vertical area at the side of the body through which the forward and backward swing is performed.
2. The frontal ('door') plane. The vertical area in front of the body through which the side-to-side swing is performed.
3. The transverse ('table') plane. The horizontal flat area around the body through which the turning swing is performed.

Swing in the 'Wheel' Plane

Holding one end in each hand, with the rope in front of your feet, swing the rope forwards stretching your arms away in front, then swing back on to the right side with your right arm sideways and your left hand coming up to your right armpit. Repeat the forward swing, then swing back on to the left side, with your left arm sideways and your right arm up to your left armpit.

Practise several swings like this, with the feet together, but relax the knees so that there is a little bend and stretch of the legs with each swing. After this, the same exercise can be done with the feet apart. As you swing forward, take a step forward on to your left foot, then transfer the weight back on to your right foot as the rope comes into your right side. Transfer the weight forward again with the next forward swing, then close your right foot up to your left to change the weight, and step back on to your left foot as you swing backwards with the rope on the left side. From then on, with each repetition you will change feet on the forward swing and step back with the other foot.

Next, try the same swinging movement forwards and backwards, feet together or feet apart, but this time with the rope folded in two, holding both knots in the same hand.

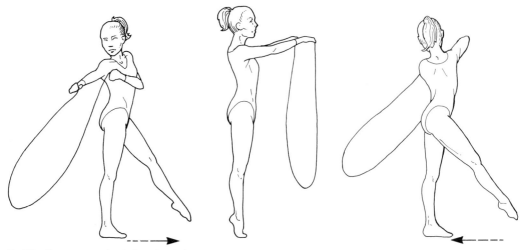

Fig 54   Open rope swing in the wheel plane.

You will soon discover that you need to change hands in order to swing to the other side of the body, but make sure that you work 'in opposition', i.e. step forwards with the left foot when the rope swings forwards in the right hand, and vice versa. Also remember to stretch the arm well forward and keep it in front even on the backward swing so that the rope does the swinging and stays in an even shape without kinking or flicking up.

Once you have mastered this simple swing (and so got the body, feet and rope moving, as well as the hand changes) it is easy to link it with some skipping. With an end in each hand, according to which way the rope is swinging, take it into:

1.   Forward or backward skipping.
2.   Half-time or single-time skipping.
3.   On the spot or travelling skipping.
4.   Combinations of the above.

Alternatively, once the rope is folded and both ends are in one hand, take the swing into a full circle at the side of the body, in either a forward or backward direction, or on both sides of the body, alternately right and left to form a figure of eight type movement. This can be combined with a body wave or a balance or can travel with a *chassé* step.

To become more adventurous, the full circle can be taken into a throw. Initially this is best done with the rope circling backwards at the side of the body, the arm held extended and slightly forwards, in front of the body (pointing diagonally forwards). The movement should be quite gentle and controlled. Once the rope is swinging, using a wrist action lower the arm slightly and then raise it upwards to release the rope when the arm is stretched to a forward and diagonally upward position. The rope will rise into the air in a folded shape, but it will open out, and the two knots will separate so that you can catch it again with one end in each hand. Do not throw the rope too vigorously as this will cause it to over-rotate. In fact, the rope needs to turn over only once as this makes the catch easier and it can be followed immediately by a forward skip. Remember what was said in the first chapter about stretching up with the arm and following through on the throw, and also reaching up with both arms to catch the rope as early and as high as possible.

Swing in the 'Door' Plane

This is the side-to-side swing, with feet apart sideways. The arms work a little like a see-saw when the rope is open.

With an end in each hand, stretch the arms sideways so that the rope hangs across the front of the feet. Sway gently from right to left, transferring the weight from one foot to the other. Lean away from the rope on each swing, i.e. when the weight is on the left foot, lean to the right and vice versa. Allow the knees to relax so that the movement is not jerky, and, most important of all, keep the arms wide apart, taking the left arm high and the right arm low as the weight moves to the left side, and then swing and change like a pendulum when the weight transfers to the other side. At all times, the rope should remain in a good curve shape; if it kinks it is probably because your arms are too close together, your movement is too jerky or you are not leaning sufficiently to one side.

As with the swing in the wheel plane, this is a basic movement which can be developed in a variety of ways. It is quite a challenge to try a turn with the body, taking the open rope swing overhead. The feet must of course move for the turn; just three little steps are all that is needed. If turning to the right first, step right–left–right and, lead-

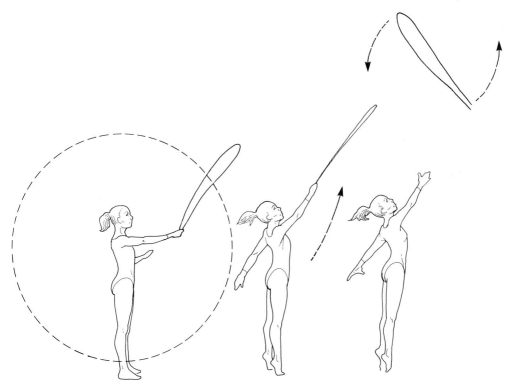

Fig 55   Swing into a throw, circling the rope backwards.

ing with the right arm, swing it up overhead, the left arm going down first to the left side, and then stretching overhead. Keep the arms wide apart, and on completion of the turn swing the right arm down across the front of the body and swing the rope across to the right side. When practising this movement, begin with a couple of side swings as a preparation, and again before repeating the turn to the other side.

Swings with the folded rope are in some ways more difficult to control since in order to prevent the rope kinking during the side-to-side swing, the arm must not only be extended forwards at shoulder height, but must also reach across to the side with each swing. Smoothness in the weight transfer through the *plié* position is absolutely essential; jerkiness causes difficulty in controlling the apparatus.

The folded rope swing in the door plane can be performed:

1. With a change of hand.
2. Leading into a full circle.
3. Leading into a throw in front of the body.
4. Into a throw under the leg.

The method of catching the rope in all these cases is up to you, as long as the basic technique of throwing and catching is adhered to and the movement is fully extended.

Swing in the 'Table' Plane

The swing of the rope in the table plane is the most difficult to execute with this apparatus, because the rope is so flexible. The sway from side to side is not practical,

Fig 56   Swing the rope well away from the body and keep it moving.

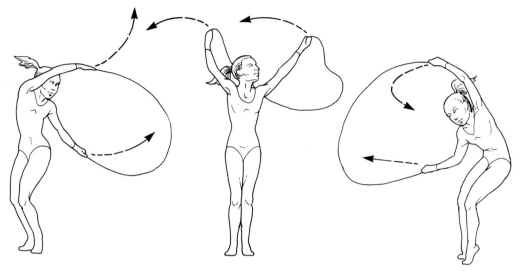

Fig 57   Half-spiral with the rope.

Fig 58   Jump high so that the body does not have to bend too far down.

Rope

although a full turn can be achieved with an open rope; this is best linked with another movement such as a half-spiral or a wrap. Both of these are basic moves, the half-spiral consisting merely of a full circle of both arms overhead and around the body, with the arms apart. If swinging to the left, take the right arm high and the left arm low out to the left side and around to the back, then drop the right arm low and bring the left arm high overhead to get the rope back to the front. Now, keeping the arms wide, and approximately at shoulder height, turn to the left and the rope will float around you.

This could be followed by a wrap. At the end of the turn, as you are returning to face forwards, place the right arm across the front of the body with the right hand on the left side of your waist and holding your left arm high in the air, circle the rope around your waist two or three times until it is 'wrapped'. To 'unwrap', swing the rope in reverse, and follow with a spiral, a turn, a wrap in the opposite direction or join the ends together to fold the rope, holding both ends in one hand and circling it overhead 'helicopter-fashion'. The helicopter swing itself can be used to swing:

1. Overhead with a balance, a bend, or travel.
2. Around the waist with a balance or steps.
3. Under the feet with a jump or leap.
4. Around the feet or legs during a shoulder stand.

These are just a few suggestions, there are many others, and you should create your own movement combinations.

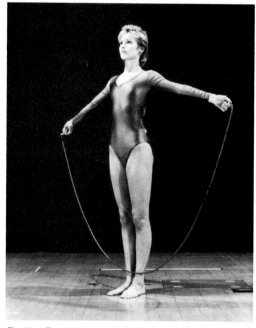

Fig 59   For this 'trap', start with the rope in front of the feet.

Fig 62   Move the left arm across the body, cross the right arm over the top of the left.

Fig 60   Swing the rope backwards, lift the right
          leg and place it over the rope.

Fig 61   Swing the arms forwards, trapping the
          rope against the left ankle.

Fig 63   Push the left arm through the rope and
          begin to move it out to the left.

Fig 64   Stretch both arms out to the side and
          pull the rope tight.

Rope

Other Movements Using the Rope

From these basic swings, we have covered movements such as circles, wraps, spirals and throws with open or folded rope, the folded rope being doubled. However, the rope is also used when folded three or four times, either to jump over, to hook up the foot into a balance, to hold momentarily around the waist or shoulders or in any other position. Again, the possibilities are wide and varied, and there is opportunity for the gymnast and coach to create their own original movements.

One other rope action which should be added to your vocabulary is the 'release'. This means that one end of the rope is thrown away whilst a grip is maintained on the other end. This is developed from an open rope swing. Probably the easiest to try first is from the side swing in the door plane. As the weight is transferred across to the right side, swing the left arm down towards the floor and at the same time let go of the end of the rope. Because you are swinging across to the right, the rope will brush the floor and swing out to the right side. As the end rises up from the floor, you can either catch it in your right hand which is already holding the other end, or you could move this from your right hand into your left before catching the free end in your right. Other possibilities for one-end releases are also quite varied; why not experiment with different swings in the different planes, or try releasing one end to swing away from you so that it drops and rises into a position for you to catch?

Sequences

The culmination of rhythmic gymnastics is a sequence, exercise, or routine, whichever you like to call it. Whether for competition, display, recreation or fitness-training, the need to link movements together is evident. For repetition practice, the phrase could be quite short with just two or three movements linked together, and if you are building towards a competition routine you should bear in mind that there may be rules that stipulate certain time restrictions. If you are devising your own choreography for display or recreation, this could be as long or as short as you like, and might possibly depend upon the music and its length, or your ability to edit it to a prescribed length.

CLASSWORK AND PARTNER WORK

Much fun can be had in a class or club where there are a number of participants, of whatever age. Children love to play skipping games: a long rope formed by tying two or three together, with two 'turners' can become quite competitive as each child strives to 'keep the kettle boiling' or jump into the rope in turn with a rhyme such as 'salt–mustard–vinegar–pepper'. Trying to get everyone into the rope and keep the skipping going can take quite some time. The one who trips over the rope usually finishes up being the turner.

Partner work is a challenge for everyone and an excellent form of practice. Some examples of this are given in the following list:

1. These involve two people skipping in one rope: one person turns the rope while both skip facing each other inside the rope; the second person turns around during the skipping; the turners are changed during the skipping; each person holds one end of the rope and turns it; the second person comes in at the back of her partner; both travel during skipping.

2. These involve two people working in unison: both perform the same sequence in time with each other either side by side or one behind the other; both perform the same sequence but on opposite sides so that they are mirroring each other (they can be face to face or back to back).

3. This involves two people working in canon: one person performs a movement and her partner repeats the identical movement immediately afterwards.

4. These involve two people using each other: to get over or under each other with folded rope; to skip together with two ropes; to wrap one rope and swing the other.

5. These involve two people exchanging apparatus: passing ropes to each other; throwing ropes to each other; one person taking two ropes, then giving one back.

With a large class of gymnasts, or even if there are only two people, many of the above ideas can be linked together. The challenge of creating a sequence, finding interesting ways of using the movements with a partner, and finding different ways of exchanging the apparatus can be quite fun and provide the basis of teaching material for children in school. There are so many possibilities that you will find the work of every pair different and equally interesting.

4 Ball

The elements of bouncing, rolling and throwing are fundamental to work with the ball, and these must be included in all exercises. The ball is the one piece of apparatus where throwing is a listed fundamental according to the Code of Points book, though it is of course common to all the other pieces too. This means that particular attention must be paid to the throwing technique and that sufficient throws of various types must be included in the final exercise. Skills common to the other pieces of apparatus – those of swinging, circling and spinning – must also be practised and included in the routine.

THROWS

For improving throwing and catching technique the ball would seem to be the obvious apparatus to use, but though we usually associate the ball with throwing and catching, the technique used in games such as netball, basketball and cricket is very different from that used in rhythmic gymnastics. The objectives are so vastly different: the games-player is aiming to keep possession of the ball within his team, and how he receives and passes the ball is of no consequence as long as it is accurate. The rhythmic gymnast on the other hand has to make the throwing and catching techniques look elegant, simultaneously performing balletic and intricate movements whilst the ball is in the air. Additionally, there are certain constraints under which the gymnast must work in competition in order to satisfy the judges, notably three rules which greatly affect the work if elements of superior difficulty are to be performed. These are:

1. The ball must be caught in one hand only, smoothly, with continuity of movement and without obvious smacking noise.
2. The left hand must be used as much as the right hand; this also applies to the throwing and catching elements.
3. One or more of the body-movement skills must be performed whilst the ball is in the air. There can be no standing or waiting as a preparation for the catch.

As with all the skills in rhythmic gymnastics the number of possible ways of performing these skills is infinite, so originality and invention are of great importance. If you are a creative coach or gymnast in terms of movement, you have a valued gift.

Look at the table opposite. Listed are different ways of throwing and catching the ball, although this is not a comprehensive list. By selecting one method of throwing and one method of catching and then varying them, and by adding a body-movement skill of your choice, you are beginning to create your own elements which, linked together, form the basis of a sequence. Before doing so, though, you should consult the table.

SUGGESTIONS FOR THROWING AND CATCHING

THROWING ACTIONS	CATCHING ACTIONS
1. Swing the arm forwards and upwards, stretching the fingers and releasing the ball by rolling it up the middle finger.	1. Reach up with the throwing arm to catch the ball above the head and swing the arm down and back with the ball (reverse of throw action).
2. Swing the arm down and back, turning the palm under and releasing the ball behind the body.	2. As above, but catch the ball with one hand in a kneeling position on the floor.
3. Swing the arm across the body from left to right and release the ball out to the right side.	3. Reach up with both arms and catch the ball in two hands, immediately bringing the ball in close to the stomach. You should have adopted a curled position.
4. With the ball placed on the backs of both hands swing the arms forward and up to release the ball off the back of the hands, keeping the arms straight.	4. Reach up to catch the ball on the backs of both hands, lower the arms with the ball as contact is made.
5. With the elbow bent and the back of the hand resting on the shoulder palm upwards, extend the arm upwards releasing the ball above the head with a push throw.	5. Reach up to catch with two hands and roll the ball up the forearms, while bending the elbows to cup the ball into the chest.
6. With the ball in two hands and the backs of the hands facing the chest as for a chest pass, push both arms upwards to send the ball above the head.	6. Place the hands behind the body at waist level, arms bent, and catch the ball behind the back.

Here are two examples of how you might select and use the various throwing and catching elements from the table above:

1. Take throwing action number 6 and catching action number 1 and perform it with a full turn: using both hands, push the ball upwards above the head, make a full turn on two feet to the left or right, keeping both arms stretched upwards, then reach with the right hand to catch the ball and swing the arm down and back as the ball is caught.

2. Take throwing action number 1 and

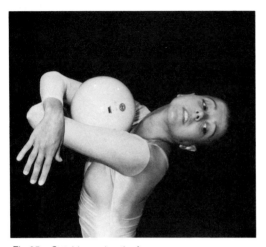

Fig 65 Catching using the forearms.

catching action number 2 and perform it with a forward roll: swing the right arm forward and up to release the ball into the throw, do a forward roll, quickly tucking one leg under to come to a kneeling position on one knee. Reach up to catch the ball with the right hand and swing the

arm down and back. (This manoeuvre demands great accuracy to ensure that the ball descends into position for the catch whilst the gymnast is kneeling on the floor.)

A number of the catches listed above are made with two hands and should be included to add variety to the overall composition of the exercise. It must be noted that in competitions judged under the international Code of Points, catches with one hand only must be included to give the highest tariff of difficulty. Whilst this is obviously more difficult to achieve with co-ordination and smoothness, it is an essential part of the technique of ball work and so should be practised and used as much as possible.

Fig 66 Variation in level and rhythm of bounces.

BOUNCES

The bouncing action is similar to that of the dribble in basketball. The hand should be supple and flexible, the ball being bounced by the fingers pressing down on to the ball with each bounce. Try not to keep the hand too rigid as it will smack on the ball and you will have difficulty in controlling it. Unlike basketball in which the aim is to retain possession and so keep the ball close to the body, in rhythmic gymnastics it is necessary to extend the arm away from the body in order to maintain a graceful line and prepare for the following move with extension and swing. The body should also be flexible and resilient, so that the knees and ankles bend with each bounce and there is a fluency about the action. Repeated bouncing, although needing to be practised in the early learning stages, soon becomes boring and a more interesting variety of bounces should be introduced. This might include the following: high, medium or low bounces; bounces using each hand; bounces using both hands; bounces using other parts of the body, such as the foot, elbow, shoulder or knee; bounces rebounding off other parts, such as the shoulder, chest or leg.

Almost anything goes, and it is worth experimenting to find your own unique trick. Indeed, many of the skills of the famous Harlem Globetrotters would be of value to the rhythmic gymnast, for instance the bouncing or passing of the ball around the body or under the legs. However, care must be taken to ensure that the bouncing can be choreographed into the most suitable part of the music. There is often a little rhythmic pattern to which a bounce or bounces will fit, and this both helps to 'highlight' the music and gives good interpretation. Small rhythmic bounces can only usually occur whilst the gymnast is stationary in a pose or

balance, but bigger bounces allow for greater body movement. Here are some for you to try:

1. One big bounce, followed by a full turn and catch before a second bounce.
2. One big bounce pushing the ball forward slightly, then a forward roll and catch.
3. Run and leap with a bounce from the right to left hand, bouncing the ball under the leg whilst in the air on the leap.
4. One big bounce, drop to one knee and catch the ball behind the body in a back-bend position.

Fig 67   Bouncing of the ball from one side to the other under the leap.

ROLLS

Both the floor and your body are the surfaces used for rolling of the ball, and whereas it is far easier to start with the rolls on the floor, much fun can be had in trying out the various rolls on the body. In every case, the rolling action must be smooth and continuous and should be performed with elegance and style. This is a particularly important consideration for the roll on the floor, for in starting it off the gymnast must bend the knees in order to get low, almost brushing the fingers along the floor, as in a normal ten-pin bowling action. This not only ensures a smooth rolling action on the floor, but also looks more elegant than having your bottom stuck up in the air!

Once the ball is set in motion any body movement may be performed before the ball is collected again. The gymnast could perform a dance step, leaps alongside or over the ball, or add a turn or a body wave as well. Try collecting the ball in a variety of different ways. Here are a few suggestions:

1. Overtake the ball and with a half-turn to face it, collect it in one hand, palm upwards.
2. Move alongside the ball and, still facing the same way, collect it with the hand facing backwards, palm upwards.
3. Overtake the ball and with a half turn

collect it with both hands together, either palms upwards or on to the backs of both hands.

It also looks quite dramatic if the pick-up goes immediately into a throw, so that the action of collecting the ball becomes the preparation for the throw itself. Practise these ideas and links and then see if you can find different ways of setting the ball off into the roll, perhaps with a different part of the body, or in a different direction. Now choose one of these movements and add it on to a little bouncing phrase and you are beginning to create your own sequence . . .

Body Rolls

Perhaps you can now begin to roll the ball on the body. This takes a little practice; some people can manage it more easily than others. One secret for success is to relax. At first, just practise rolling the ball from the hand along the arm to shoulder level. If you

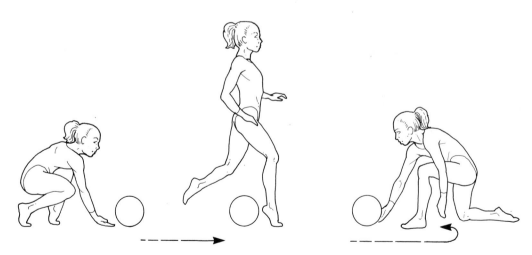

Fig 68   Bend low to roll and receive the ball to effect a fluent movement.

are right-handed, use the left hand to stop the ball by the chin and push it back down the right arm again. One important teaching point; do not flick the fingers or wrist upwards to initiate the roll up the arm as this is considered bad technique. Instead, open the fingers and push the whole arm away from the body, at the same time lifting the hand slightly above shoulder level. This will start the ball rolling without having to make any positive effort with the hand. Once the roll up and down the right arm is mastered, try the same with the left hand. Finally, make a full chest roll by rolling the ball up the right arm, across the chest and down the left arm, or vice versa. To achieve a successful chest roll, keep both arms in a forward diagonal position rather than completely sideways. This prevents the ball from rolling off the hands at the end, and gives a better line and better control. Also, drop the head back slightly or turn it so that the chin is not in the way! There are some other body rolls for you to try:

1. With the right hand, place the ball against the stomach or chest and pull the hand upwards to start the ball rolling up the chest and over the right shoulder. Curl forwards a little, allowing the ball to roll down the back and catch it behind at waist level with one or both hands.
2. Sit in a 'long sitting position' – legs together and out straight in front – place the ball on the ankles and pull with the fingers to roll it up the legs to the lap. Then push away with the fingers to roll it back down the legs. On the next go, lie down as the ball rolls up the legs, and see if you can continue the roll right up the body. Alternatively, this movement can be done in reverse by starting lying down with the ball at chest level. Eventually, you might be able to incorporate a roll through the arms as well as the body.

Any part of the body can be used for rolling the ball, and as body rolls are a fundamental requirement for work with the ball, some of these must be included in an exercise. Different kinds of rolls should be included, and a new rule applying to top level work states that there should be at least one roll along the whole length of the body.

OTHER MOVEMENTS WITH THE BALL

Other movements to include in the exercise must be those of swinging, circling, and spiralling. These skills are difficult to perform with the ball as it is not easy to control the apparatus without holding it. A grip with the fingers is not permitted, neither is a hooking of the wrist to hold the ball against the forearm (called 'cupping'). At all times, the ball should be balanced freely on the hand with the fingers extended. When performing a swing in a backwards direction,

Fig 69 The 'seal' – rolling the body over the ball on the floor.

the arm is turned outwards so that the ball can remain balanced on the hand without being gripped by the fingers. In spiralling or twisting the ball over or under the body, the palm needs to remain upwards, the movement made large and with full extension, and the ball kept well away from the body.

Finally, let us consider the simple movement of spinning, easily performed when the ball is placed on the floor. With fingers on top of the ball and spread wide, give a twist or flick of the wrist in a circular motion to set the ball spinning on the spot – like a top. During this action, the gymnast can show almost any of the body-movement skills, for she is free of the ball. This is quite permissable, provided that both gymnast and apparatus are working, and that you can find your own way of getting into and out of the movement. You might like to develop this idea a little further, and try to make the ball spin on the fingers, even on one finger, or on another part of the body. This becomes quite tricky and needs a great deal of practice to perfect, especially when you try to link it with a body element.

Sequences

In constructing a sequence, however long, consideration must be given to the inclusion of all the characteristic movements of the apparatus. Therefore, with the ball you should ensure that you include spins, swings, circles, spirals, bounces, rolls and throws. As well as these, the body elements must be shown, though how the two are linked is up to each individual gymnast and her coach. It is this linkage or combination of elements which presents the opportunity for the creation of such a wide and varied programme within the sport, and which provides excellent teaching material for teachers and children.

CLASSWORK

As with the rope, much fun can be had by using the ball for play and at the same time allowing for practice and improvement of general handling skills with the apparatus. Many of the practices used in the games lesson can be adapted and brought to life if used within the rhythmic gymnastics lesson with some music added to it. For teaching or recreational purposes, there is absolutely no reason why pop music should not be used, and as the youth of today are particularly *au fait* with the charts, why not practise some of the skills to music from the 'Top Twenty'? Start with some bounces:

1.   Bounce the ball on the spot to the right of the body with the right hand. Once a steady rhythm is established, skip around the ball in a clockwise direction whilst maintaining the bounces on the spot. Repeat with the left hand on the left side, and skip in an anticlockwise direction. Now link the two together: eight bounces and skips to the right and eight to the left (any two or four-beat music can be used for this: an excellent piece is the BBC TV *Rugby Special* signature tune).
2.   Bouncing the ball on the spot in front of the body with one or both hands, make two medium bounces and three small bounces, counting one–two, one–two–three or one–two, cha-cha-cha (this can also be performed to the music suggested above, or to any 'cha-cha' music).
3.   With a travelling polka step forwards, i.e. hop–step–close–step with the right foot leading, then with the left foot leading, perform two bounces of the ball with each polka step. There are two points to note here – use the opposite hand to foot, so that when the right foot leads into the polka step

bounce the ball with the left hand, then change hands as the left foot leads; also, place the ball in front of the feet when bouncing, and push it forwards slightly to enable the forward travelling to take place without the ball landing on the feet (similar music again can be used here).

These bouncing exercises are quite good fun to perform in time with the music, and also act as warming-up activities at the beginning of a class session. Practice of some simple rolls could follow:

Sitting on the floor, roll the ball forwards, backwards, sideways, pushing it away from the body and bringing it back again, using the fingertips and keeping the movement continuous. Next, push it further away by lying down, then begin to roll it under the body, perhaps under the leg in a kneeling position, under both legs in a 'V-sit position', or under the body in a back-arch position. Now keep changing the body position, and the direction of the ball, so there is constant movement of ball and body. Many ideas can develop from this, which serves to introduce to beginners the rolling action allied with some body movement. Make sure the ball is touched lightly with the fingers rather than hand or wrist (this again can be done to music, of a slower nature, perhaps a pop ballad or some of Richard Clayderman's piano music).

The rolling action can be used as an easy introduction to exchanges with the ball in partner work. Here are a few suggestions, along with other ways of exchanging the ball:

1.   Two people facing each other in a kneeling position about 3m apart roll the ball to each other and do a full spin turn on the knees or bottom or do a backward roll before receiving the ball from their partner.

2.   Two people, standing facing each other and apart, each roll the ball out to the right diagonal side, then do a quarter left turn, run and leap or do a forward roll to collect the ball from their partner.

3.   Two people, standing facing each other and apart as above, perform the above element but throwing the ball instead of rolling it.

4.   Two people, standing side by side and close, both throw the ball straight up in the air, change places with each other and catch the partner's ball. (Remember to decide beforehand who goes in front and who behind!)

5.   Two people, facing each other and about 8m apart, bounce the ball towards each other, perform a forward roll and catch the ball from their partner after one bounce.

6.   Two people, moving towards each other, run lightly with the ball balanced on the outstretched right hand. When close and facing, they begin to wheel about each other, and pass the ball into their partner's left hand. Look at the ball you are receiving then spin away from each other. This can be done in a back-to-back position also, and looks very effective when performed smoothly.

Having experimented with some of the exchanges listed above, and got an idea of the possibilities of exchanging with rolls, throws, passes or bounces, you can begin to find some more ways of your own. Each pair in a class could be set the task of selecting two exchanges of their own choice, linking them together with three other movements in between which they are asked to travel with steps or leaps, perform a balance and also a turn. This work involves certain body elements, but the

Ball

gymnasts are permitted to use the ball in any way they wish, so there is plenty of opportunity for them to think out and apply their own ideas.

5 Hoop

Two elements – rolling and rotation – are listed as fundamentals of hoop work, though there are more possibilities for variation of apparatus manipulation with the hoop than with any other piece. Though it is large in comparison with other pieces of apparatus, its solidity and form make it fairly easy for beginners to handle, although at times it can prove difficult to keep in plane or to change planes. Swings and circles, turning over, passing through, and throwing are additional characteristics of hoop work and all play an important part in the finished sequence.

As with the rope, the grip on the hoop should be light so that the various manipulations may be performed with smoothness and dexterity, although occasionally – when preparing for some of the throws, for instance – the grip will need to be very firm. The two types of grip used are the overgrasp (hand on the outside of the hoop, fingers curled around it) and the undergrasp (hand inside the hoop, palm upwards as if hanging the hoop on the hand).

The thumb and fingers play a vital part in all the various skills involving the use of the hand or hands. As with the other apparatus, work must be performed in the left hand as well as the right, so it is essential that when learning a skill it is practised in both hands.

The element of rotation, in which the hoop spins around a hand or other part of the body must not be confused with the turnover of the hoop. This is also a spinning action, but around a long axis extending from one outer edge of the hoop to the other, rather like a spinning coin.

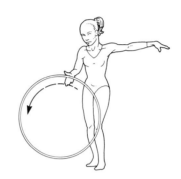

Fig 70   Rotation with arm forwards.

ROTATION

As mentioned, various parts of the body are used to show the rotating hoop in action, the most common of which is the hand, and this is where the beginner can start to learn the action. The hoop is rotated between the thumb and the forefinger, and should be worked initially with the arm outstretched in front of the body at shoulder height. The arm and wrist will move up and down very slightly to aid the rotation and an opening and closing of the fingers will give added control, as well as provide a more relaxed action. Try to avoid holding the hand in a rigid position with the thumb stuck up in the air! It should not take long to achieve this rotation on the hand, and fairly quick progress can be made towards some of the other skills listed below:

1.   Whilst rotating the hoop on the outstretched hand in front, link with travelling steps – first walk forwards, then backwards.

Hoop

Next run, skip, polka or *pas de bas* forwards, then backwards.

2.   Begin the rotation again with the hoop in
front of the body, then make a quarter turn
so that the hoop is rotating at the side of the
body in the wheel plane. Now add some of
the travelling movements described above
or perform some dance steps on the spot.

3.   Place the hoop around the waist and,
setting off the spin with the hands, perform
the hula-hoop rotation. This looks effective
when performed with a balance on the toes
of one foot – or a few running steps.

4.   From a sitting position, roll back and up
on to the shoulders with the feet inside the
hoop, at the same time using the hands to
initate a rotation on the feet, ankles or legs.

5.   Still with the rotation in front of the body,

Fig 72   Concluding the rotation with a catch
and balance.

Fig 71   Using the foot for rotation.

*Figs 73–74   Development from kneeling to standing
becomes more difficult.*

Fig 74

lower the arm gently and stretch upwards, releasing the hoop with a throw above the head (feel the hoop spin off the side of the index finger).

For this last throw, the arm stretches upwards with a good follow-through so that the hoop rises vertically above the head. By placing the hand back inside the hoop on its descent, it is possible to return immediately to the rotation. Once the correct technique and control over the direction of the throw has been mastered with the arm forward, then the same skill can be tried with the hoop in the wheel plane.

For the throw in the wheel plane, the arm is placed in a forward diagonal position rather than a true sideways position to enable an easy and controllable action. It is essential that the arm is fully stretched both during the preparatory rotation and for the throw itself, and that you have a strong follow-through of the arm on the release. It is not necessary to swing the arm violently or to bend it to achieve a good high throw – a gentle lowering and lifting of the arm will do.

The catch is more difficult in this position because of the backward spin of the hoop, and the hand needs to reach inside the hoop at the lower front edge if the rotation action is to be continued. Alternatively, try a simple overgrasp catch bringing the hoop down at the side with a swing.

ROLLING

Rolling along the floor demands care in setting the hoop off into the roll so that it remains vertical and in a straight line. When it is in motion, the gymnast performs a variety of body movements, having to travel at some stage to catch up with it and collect it. More exciting movements involve leaping

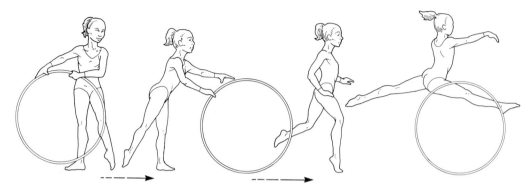

Fig 75   Simple roll and leap beside the hoop.

over the hoop, diving or rolling through it and kicking it up into the air.

A further option is for the gymnast to put back-spin on to the hoop so that it returns like a boomerang, so allowing more static movements to be performed during the roll away and return. In order to achieve this, the arm must be swung vigorously forwards to achieve the roll away, but the wrist pulls up and back equally vigorously in order to put the back-spin on to the hoop. This is fun to do, and creates great amusement when the action is not quite true, and the hoop rolls off towards someone else instead of coming back to the sender!

Of greater difficulty, because of the size of the hoop, is the roll on the body. The technique is basically the same as that used for rolling the ball (identical for the actual roll itself), but the difference lies in initiating the movement. The hoop must be gripped more tightly to ensure that it is placed in a vertical position on the body. The fingers open and the hand pushes away as with the ball, though pressing down on the hoop with the thumb helps to set the hoop in motion. Having mastered the chest roll and the shoulder roll with the ball, it is suggested that you try these straightaway with the hoop, then perhaps add the roll from one hand to the other across the back of the shoulders.

SWINGING

The basic swinging action with the hoop is particularly important as a preparation for

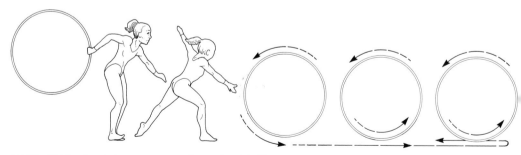

Fig 76   The back-spin boomerang requires quite a lot of force.

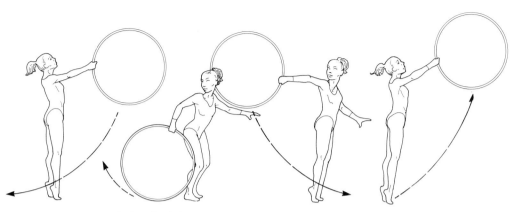

Fig 77   Simple swinging in the wheel plane.

the throws, as well as being an intricate part of the manipulations of this apparatus. The hoop lends itself to a wide variety of ways of throwing and catching, and these develop from swings in the various planes, with one hand or with both. A forward–backward swing at the side of the body with the hoop held in overgrasp in the right hand is the first swing to use for throwing. It can be done with feet together or feet apart, 'changing' hands and feet in the same way as the exercise described with the rope (*see* page 43). The technique differs again due to the size and solidity of the hoop; because the arm should remain almost fully stretched (though *not* rigid) in order to prevent the hoop hitting the floor as it swings past the leg, the body leans away slightly from the swinging arm. Also, the arm is held away from the body a little to allow for more freedom of the swing. Unlike the rope where the action is mostly brought about through the wrist, the swing occurs through the shoulder joint and so the whole arm is used.

As the hoop reaches the peak of its forward swing, it can be released into the vertical throw, gently at first, to acquire good control and direction, and then gradually increasing in height and strength until the hoop soars up to, but does not touch, the ceiling. The catch is a simple reverse procedure; stretch up with the arm and make contact as early as possible with the outside edge of the hoop, fingers in overgrasp, then continue the downward swing of both arm and hoop together. The position and plane of the hoop is identical to that described in the rotation throw. Either throw can be caught as suggested above, or the rotation catch can be used, with the hand reaching inside to the lower, front edge of the hoop as it descends. You will notice that whichever type of throw is used, a backward rotation is placed upon the hoop when it is thrown and this rotation must continue in the same direction for the rotation catch.

The hoop also lends itself particularly well to swings in the table plane, initially using two hands, but then progressing to one-handed swings. A strong grip is needed to hold the hoop in a horizontal position during the basic side-to-side swings, but once you begin to develop the swing and go into a turn or change of hands, either in front or behind, the hoop becomes easier to manage. For this type of swing where the hoop is horizontal, a very different throwing action is required, and by using either one or both hands and a slight tilt of the hoop on to a diagonal plane, the discus throw can be achieved. When you have tried this throw a few times, and are becoming quite accurate, perhaps you can begin to try some different ways of catching, for example:

1. Reach up with one hand and catch on the outer edge, then step immediately into a turn.
2. Catch with both hands, bring the hoop down around the waist, and send it into a hula-hoop rotation.
3. Reach forwards and catch with one or both hands, then swing the hoop down in front of the body and skip through it.
4. Stand underneath the descending hoop and bend down to place the fingers lightly on the floor, lifting one leg high at the back and letting the hoop drop like a hoop-la over the extended leg and body. (This body position is called a front scale and is similar to a very deep arabesque.)

Fig 78   Variation of the catch from a flat throw.

The last swing to be mentioned, in the door plane, allows for further variety of movement. From the side-to-side swing can develop: a change of hand in front or overhead; a rotation in front or at the side of the body; a throw overhead; or simply a quarter-turn to change direction and plane.

Having considered the swing and how it is used and developed with other apparatus, and by injecting your own ideas and innovations, the possibilities for movement ideas once again become quite numerous. This also applies to other actions like the turn-over, and getting through the hoop, and having already suggested that the rhythmic gymnastics apparatus is fun to 'play' with, these are two characteristic movements which are just that. Try some of the following:

1. Stand the hoop vertically on the floor, spin it with the thumb and fingers and run round it or perform a body wave before collecting it. Watch its spinning action carefully, and turn the wrist and fingers in the same direction as the hoop is spinning in order to regrasp it.
2. Holding the hoop with both hands apart and underneath the outside edge, lower the arms and then swing them upwards into a throw, releasing the hoop so that it turns over on itself when in the air.
3. With one or both hands holding the hoop, using either undergrasp or overgrasp, skip forwards or backwards through it. Perform some skips on the spot, then begin to travel.
4. From a kneeling position on the floor with the hoop held horizontally overhead in both hands, bend both arms and lower the hoop down over the body, then sit back through the hoop and roll backwards into a shoulder-stand, stretching upwards with the arms and bringing the apparatus out over the feet.

5.   Using a throw and catch of your choice – and that you feel is suitable – immediately jump through the hoop on catching it. Though not under separate headings, many of the throwing elements have been dealt with in combination with other actions and particularly in connection with the swinging action. The importance of preparation must be realised before throwing any apparatus, and similarly a follow-through at the end of the throw. These are techniques which apply in general when throwing any object. The direction of the swing and the moment of release of the apparatus determine its flight path, and because the rhythmic gymnast is looking for a variety of different flight paths, according to the movement elements which are being performed underneath the apparatus, much practice of both the throw and catch, as well as of the body movements, is vital. In every case, even with the simplest of skills, the body element and the apparatus element must be practised both separately and together in order to achieve the final harmonious movement.

Sequences

Of particular importance when creating a sequence is the change of plane of the apparatus; this is a major factor for consideration with the hoop because of its bulkiness. There must be variety in the use of the different planes (indeed this is stated in the judging rules), and it is worth spending time in devising and practising suitable linking movements so that the change from one plane to another can be performed without interruption to the flow of the movement. This can be achieved in the following ways:

1.   Stop the motion of the hoop and check it in a suitable pose or balance position, then recommence in a different plane.
2.   Turn the body through a quarter of a turn, so changing the hoop from the wheel to the door plane, or vice versa.
3.   Release the hoop, i.e. let go of it by throwing, rolling or spinning, and collect it with immediate change of plane.

Figs 78–81   Different check positions preceding a change of plane.

Hoop

Fig 80

Fig 81

These three factors also apply to plane changes with other apparatus and by ensuring that each plane is used, you will automatically include a variety of apparatus manipulations.

CLASSWORK

There will be times when insufficient apparatus is available for a whole class or group to work with a piece each. Whatever the apparatus, it is perfectly possible to achieve adequate work and practice with two people sharing one piece. Sometimes – even when there is enough equipment available – it is practical in the learning stages of exchanges with a partner to practise with one piece of apparatus between two people. In this situation, the gymnast only has to concentrate on one action at a time, for example either the throw or the catch. This also provides the opportunity to concentrate a little more on the body-work and ensure that some of the movement skills are included in between or during the exchange. The following are some ideas for work with one piece of apparatus between two:

1. Throw, roll or pass the hoop to your partner whilst facing each other at a distance. Perform a turn, a balance or a back-bend whilst waiting for the return of the hoop.
2. Standing side by side, throw the hoop up and forward, your partner then performs a forward roll to stand and catch the hoop.
3. Standing apart, roll the hoop towards your partner who straddle-jumps or star-jumps over it and immediately turns to collect it.
4. Standing facing and close together, place the hoop over your partner's head as in hoop-la, then let go of it as your partner

Fig 82   A basic exchange in twos.

Figs 83–85   Ideas for working with a partner.

Fig 84

Fig 85

catches and places the hoop around her waist in a hula-hoop.

5. As above, but keep hold of the hoop; your partner then steps, jumps or rolls out of it.

6. Hold the hoop on the floor or in the air for your partner to jump or roll through it.

7. Standing apart from each other, throw the hoop horizontally and flat in an attempt to 'hula-hoop' your partner, who catches it before it hits the floor.

8. Stand facing each other, both holding the hoop with two hands, and, swinging the hoop to the side and overhead, turn under the hoop simultaneously.

Beginning from these suggested movements, the teacher (or the class) can think out their own ideas for working together with a partner. Having watched other members of the class, and selected the best ideas, perhaps everyone could try them, then going on to linking the best moves together.

6 Ribbon

To pick up the ribbon and stick and swing it about in the various planes to create a variety of patterns is suprisingly easy – anyone can do it – provided that the correct swivel attachment between ribbon and stick is used, and that the performer stands still! Once the body movements are incorporated, particularly turning and travelling, the low level and the more advanced movements, the risk of getting tangled in the ribbon becomes much greater. The emphasis throughout rhythmic gymnastics is upon harmony between body and apparatus movement, and the ribbon is no exception – indeed it is this which makes the work with the ribbon particularly difficult.

Continuity is all-important, for the ribbon must not 'die'. It is long, light and flexible and must be worked throughout its entire length. Beginners and young gymnasts do not always find it easy to sustain the work; it not only requires co-ordination and stamina, but also concentration. However, it still proves to be the most popular piece, for it gives an immediate sense of satisfaction and achievement, is fun to do and is spectacular.

The fundamental elements of ribbon-work are listed as swings, circles, snakes and coils, with additional elements of figures of eight and throws. Basically the technique is concerned with two types of action:

Fig 86   Large swinging movement on the left and right side of the body.

Ribbon

1. Large swinging movements involving the use of the whole arm, and resulting in the formation of sweeping curved patterns with the ribbon.

2. Small wrist movements, either up and down, or 'stirring', resulting in the formation of small folds (snakes) or little circles (coils) of the ribbon.

The stick is held in a natural position between the thumb and forefinger, with a fairly firm grip. This provides the usual situation for ribbon work, though occasionally part of the actual ribbon is held as well. In seeking alternative methods of manipulating the ribbon in order to give added variety and excitement, gymnasts are now using it in quite unusual ways – holding the end, the middle, folding it, stepping on it, starting with it rolled up and so on. All these different ideas must of course be built into the overall sequence, and performed with elegance and style.

SWINGS AND CIRCLES

The swings and circles follow the same format as those using the other apparatus. A clear distinction between the planes is important, and in order to show the movement and the pattern in its entirety, full extension of the body movement is vital. The arm should be stretched and the circling action large so that the ribbon describes a complete pattern away from the body. A bent arm or incomplete movement very often results in a tangle around the body or a knot in the ribbon. Equally, the movements should be unhurried to prevent an 'overtaking' of one part of the ribbon by another. Swings can be practised and developed in each of the planes as follows:

1. Door plane. Swing from side to side, the arm moving down from your right side and up to the left side, then down and back up to right side. Take the swing into a full circle with a change of hand overhead. Transfer the weight from one foot to the other whilst performing the side swings, then perform the step–close–step *(chassé)* action with the feet during the full circle.

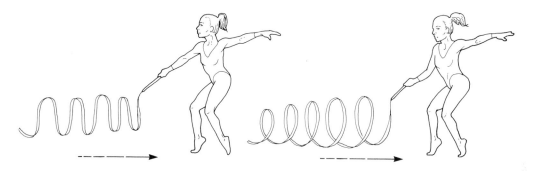

Fig 87   Small snakes and coils.

2. Table plane. With the same weight transfer from side to side as before, swing the arm across the body at shoulder height, keeping the arm swing horizontal, as if brushing the top of a high table. After two preparation swings go into a full turn, allowing the ribbon to float horizontally around the body.

3. Wheel plane. Travel forwards with walking or running steps whilst circling the arm backwards, first on the right, then on the left side, so forming a large vertical figure of eight shape with the ribbon.

With each of these swings, a hand change may be added, either in front of or behind the body, overhead, or under the leg. Try to avoid the cracking sound of the ribbon, which will be apparent if the swing is either too vigorous or snatched.

Snakes and Coils

These intricate little movements add interest and a definite change of pattern, an essential part of a ribbon sequence. The snaking action is easiest, involving an up-and-down or side-to-side movement of the wrist, depending upon which way the hand is held. The 'horizontal waterfall' is an effective snake pattern achieved by holding the arm high in front, with the stick pointing downwards, and the hand working from side to side. Though not quite so easy, this movement can also be performed behind the back, with the arm still stretching high, the wrist dropped backwards and the same side-to-side action. Combine the back waterfall with a backward arch and a few running steps forward, followed by a continuous snake over the top of the head into a front waterfall performed with a balance on one leg. This forms a logical little phrase of movement and is both enjoyable and chal-

Fig 88   Back waterfall taken into a back-bend.

lenging to perform.

By stretching the arm forwards and low and by again working the wrist from side to side, a different form of horizontal snake-pattern can be seen when you move backwards with some springing or dance steps.

The vertical snake-pattern can only be made apparent when the arm is moved across the body from side to side as the wrist is workiing up and down. Alternatively, it can be made more effective when performing a turn or when travelling forwards while snaking the ribbon up and down behind the body. However, whichever element is being performed, the technique must be quite correct.

'During all the specific ribbon elements, the apparatus must always remain well developed in space, and the shape of the pattern must be exact, precise and clearly visible. The whole length of the ribbon must participate in the pattern.

The movements must be performed energetically and continuously so that the ribbon is always in motion, remains in space and never droops.'

(International Gymnastics Federation, *Code of Points* (RSG Committee, 1982), p. 70.)

In order for the pattern of the ribbon to be clearly visible, the *Code of Points* rule further states that snakes must have a minimum of five or six loops, and that these loops must be the same size as each other. This also applies to the little circles present in the coils; these are more difficult to maintain because the 'stirring' action of the hand requires a certain degree of flexibility in the wrist joint, together with the ability to keep the circling action full and even. Continuous coils, during practice at least, can become very tiring, as the arm has to be held out away from the body, and the wrist has to work quite vigorously. As a break, try coiling the ribbon with the stick in the left hand and change direction in order to perform both outward and inward coils.

Once the basic action has been achieved, it should be combined with a body-movement skill; this is easier said than done. It can prove quite difficult to co-ordinate the fine skill of circling the wrist with a large motor skill such as a run or a leap, and even more difficult to control the free arm and its movement. Generally speaking, the free arm should be worked in opposition to the apparatus arm, but a conscious effort has to be made to involve it in the total movement otherwise it tends to hang at the side – rather like a dead fish. The free arm should be used to give the finishing touches to the 'line' of the gymnast, as understood in balletic terms, and a variety of elegant positions of this arm should be tried and practised.

Throws

The ribbon and stick throw is the most difficult of all. Because of its lightness, it is difficult to project into the air, and even if the throw is achieved with some success, determining its flight path creates even more of a problem for the inexperienced gymnast. It is only in recent years that the technique of throwing the ribbon rather than the stick has developed and this has generally proved to be more successful.

By holding the ribbon near to its attachment to the stick (in any case not more than 50cm away from it), the stick can be swung around with some speed and force, providing the necessary momentum for the throw to occur. If the stick is to be thrown, a large arm-swing is necessary to achieve any lift because the length of the ribbon and the fact that it trails on the floor slow down the action. The direction of the throw is really immaterial. The arm may circle forwards in the wheel plane, rather like a bowling action in cricket, but the release of the stick must be high overhead on the upward swing. Alternatively, the arm can circle backwards, the stick again being released at the top of the upward swing, so that the ribbon is thrown behind the body. This is perhaps a little easier than the forward swing, provided the gymnast is not too eager to turn and watch the ribbon in the air. The throwing action should be completed before the body is turned; otherwise the direction of the throw will be affected.

Sequences

Movement combinations with the ribbon are easier to create than with any other piece of apparatus because of the flexibility of the ribbon. Changes from large swinging and circling movements to small snakes or coils require little effort, but they do need to be made frequently to provide variation in the composition of a sequence, as long as each pattern is seen to be obvious before the change. Work using both hands must be evident, as must changes from one hand to the other (sometimes quite quickly) as well as changes from right to left and back again; at other times the ribbon must remain in the left hand for a much longer phrase of movement. In addition to this (not forgetting the inclusion of all the body elements plus the apparatus characteristics) some other considerations for the construction of a sequence should include: a change of level; change of direction and speed; use of the floor area and interpretation of the music.

Improvisation

The ribbon is an ideal piece of apparatus for improvisation in the early stages. Without worrying about the inclusion of the technical detail and barring any self-consciousness, the gymnast can move freely to whatever music is played and attempt to express the qualities and rhythms of the music. This is a useful exercise as it helps to build confidence: it helps the gymnast to feel and understand ways of linking movements together; it helps to develop a sense of rhythm and allows opportunity for the gymnast to seek out the kinds of movement and qualities which best fit the music used; finally, if improvisation is practised at intervals, it serves to train the performer to

Fig 89   Cheeky improvisation.

continue through a taught exercise which she has, unfortunately, temporarily forgotten!

It is also necessary to show some change in the movement and in the music, either by a change of tempo, change of rhythm, or change of style. In a full length individual sequence, which should last between sixty and ninety seconds, one could expect to hear three differing phrases. The usual format, and which is perhaps a little common now is the 'sandwich'. An example of this would be a strong and fast opening section, a slow phrase in the middle, and a return to a strong and fast last part leading up to the end. Other arrangements are now becoming evident, though, and along with the great variety of movement potential, there is plenty of room to be innovative with the music although this could, of course, prove difficult to acquire.

Cutting and editing of music from record or tape is extremely time-consuming and requires if not a certain expertise, at least some good equipment on which to do it. Alternatively, a musician may be hired to arrange and play pieces of the required length and with the necessary changes incorporated – this could perhaps be a member of the school music department. The third option is to purchase cassettes with pre-recorded music especially arranged, timed and played for rhythmic gymnastics. Quite a wide selection is now available; *see* page 120 for details.

Once the opportunity for improvisation has been given, the sequence must begin to take on a more positive and identifiable format. As movements are put together, they must be learned and repeated, adapted, changed (if necessary) until the final sequence is satisfactory and is ready to be practised both in parts and as a whole.

CLASSWORK

You will quickly realise that ribbon work *en masse* requires a considerable amount of space, posing problems for full class participation if numbers are large or if space is limited. If conditions allow, the ideal is for each gymnast to have a ribbon, but as an alternative two people could share the apparatus, as suggested in the previous chapter. Some individual 'tricks' for practice might be:

1. Holding the stick in the right hand, circle the arm forwards in the wheel plane, first on the right, then on the left side (a figure of eight). As the arm swings down on the right side, step to the side with the right foot stepping over the ribbon which is brushing past on the floor, then close the left foot to the right. Repeat the movement several times, stepping to the side with the right foot and closing the left foot to the right foot each time.

2. Hold the stick in the right hand and the other end of the ribbon in the left hand, about one foot from the end, with the arms sideways and ribbon in front. Swing the right arm forward and overhead to take the ribbon round to the back of the body and immediately start to run lightly around in a large curve so that the ribbon floats behind. Now add your own leap or snake the ribbon by working the right hand up and down. Get out by letting go of the end, or by dropping the right arm low and in front, swinging the left arm overhead whilst still holding the end of the ribbon.

3. With the stick held in the right hand, circle the ribbon overhead inwards, then down in front of the body, pointing the wrist downwards (a figure of eight above and below). During the circle below, jump with

both feet into the 'hole' made by the ribbon.

4. Holding the stick in the right hand, swing the arm quite quickly from side to side across the front of the body so that the ribbon brushes across the floor in front of the feet. Begin to travel forwards with little running steps, springing over the ribbon with each step.

5. Try a throw using either the stick or the ribbon, do a forward roll and stand up to catch.

Fig 90   Large circles of the ribbon together with good elevation are essential here.

Partner Work

Exchanges with the ribbon are extremely difficult, and not recommended for the beginner for obvious reasons. Local competitions involving partner or group work usually make it clear in the rules that throwing exchanges are not necessary, though one or two passing exchanges should be included. The problem still arises in keeping the ribbon in motion during the exchange, as well as avoiding a tangle between the two ribbons! Two very basic exchanges are:

1. You and your partner move toward each other with a circle of the ribbon overhead, stick in the right hand. Just before meeting, stretch the right arm to the side, pass the ribbon stick into your partner's left hand and then immediately turn away from each other with a snaking action. Timing is very important with the pair working closely together; the whole phrase should show continuity and flow.

2. Both partners coil the ribbon, with the stick in the right hand. One of you holds a balance position, while the other moves in and passes her ribbon into her partner's left hand. Immediately, the receiver makes a half-turn to her right, and passes her own ribbon into her partner's right or left hand, and she moves quickly away, both still maintaining the coiling action of the ribbon, if possible. Though this exchange of apparatus is not simultaneous, it is permissable so long as the two pieces are exchanged one after the other and there is no intermediary element.

There are many possibilities for working in combination with a partner and an exploitation of the 'relationship' idea will give many interesting combinations: the two gymnasts consider the various positions and places which they can adopt in relation to their partner, such as: side by side; facing each other; back to back; one behind the other; far apart; one high, one low. These possibilities provide a variety of situations in which the gymnasts can work, but there are further combinations (getting over or under each other, working in unison or canon, meeting and parting, for example); the options seem limitless.

The teacher or coach perhaps needs to set the framework for the construction of a

Ribbon

sequence; the task given will, of course, depend upon the age and the level of the gymnasts, and the length of the sequence to be performed, but a suggestion might be that the pair should work in unison, show two different relationships, and include one exchange.

7 Clubs

The clubs are by far the most difficult apparatus to work. The fact that two clubs are used simultaneously means that the gymnast must be as dextrous with the left hand as the right and must be able to co-ordinate the movement of two hands. Recent additions to the regulations stipulate the inclusion of asymmetric movements with the clubs, which require not only a high degree of co-ordination and control, but also thorough concentration. Without these attributes, attempts at some of the skills, particularly the throwing and juggling elements, can be positively dangerous. For these reasons, and bearing in mind that youngsters will immediately want to start throwing the apparatus if presented with it, it is not recommended that beginners tackle the clubs, at least not until some experience has been gained with the other apparatus, and a certain level of skill has been accomplished.

Fig 91 Asymmetric juggle

Figs 92–94 Difficult juggles require practice and ability.

Fig 93

Fig 94

The fundamental element of clubs work is the mills (small circles) and along with a simple swinging and circling action this could form the basis of introductory work for beginners.

SWINGS

The weight and shape of the clubs makes them an ideal apparatus for swinging. Indeed the origin of club swinging as an exercise in its own right dates back to the beginnings of gymnastics, when regimented exercises with dumb-bells and small clubs formed part of the 'drill' activities of the late 1800s. Club swinging as a mass participation event was very popular at one stage and in fact is still performed in some countries, notably Japan, from where groups of

male gymnasts have given displays of this art with immaculate precision and timing.

The movements are quite simple, the clubs being held tightly between the thumb and the forefinger and in line with the arm, there being little wrist movement which would cause the club to droop or lift. The arm is kept straight and the swings come from the shoulder joint, with the clubs remaining as an extension of the arm. Here are a few different swings which can be practised:

1. Standing with the feet together, and with one club in each hand, swing the arms alternately, one arm forwards and one arm backwards (wheel plane).
2. Continue the above swing into a full circle of the arms, with the arms passing each other overhead. As the arms are going

Fig 95   Alternate forward and backward
swings are basic, but become more
difficult when taken into a full circle.
overhead.

in opposite directions, this is quite difficult, especially if the shoulder joint is not very supple! However, it is a good mobility exercise and you should try to swing the arms up as close to the ears as possible. When you have mastered the full circle, try some of the forward and backward swings as preparation, and then move forward with three walking steps during the full arm circle.

3.   Standing with feet apart sideways, one club in each hand, both arms stretched out to left side, left arm at shoulder height, right arm just below. Swing arms down in front of the body then up and out to the right side, transferring the weight from the left foot to the right foot. Repeat to the other side, trying to keep the clubs in a parallel position with both arms straight, though the arm crossing the body will of necessity bend just a little.

4.   Continue the above swing into a full circle overhead, with both arms circling together and parallel, and the feet performing a sideways *chassé* step: step–close–step.

5.   Stand as in 3 above, but with both arms at shoulder height. Swing the arms horizontally across the front of the body and out to the other side, transferring the weight across from left to right and ending with a slight twist of the body to the right. Try to maintain the parallel position of the clubs in the table plane.

6.   The swing described above, as with all swings in the table plane, flows naturally into a turn, but when working with the clubs a slight adjustment of the arm position is required to give the correct line and feeling for the turn. As the turn to the right commences, swing the right arm across and out to the right side at shoulder height, keeping the left arm in position, so creating an 'open' line with both arms extended sideways. Perform the right turn with the arms in this position, then on completion of the turn and as the weight is transferred to the right side, bring the left arm across to join the right arm on the right side. (As a point of safety, you should make sure that there is plenty of room around you to turn with your arms fully extended sideways.)

It should be noted at this point that although there are a number of different swinging actions, they should not all be attempted in one go. The shoulders can become quite sore, and certainly the arms will start to ache if they are not accustomed to this sort of work. Practice of small circles (mills) involving a wrist and finger action can serve as a relief from the large shoulder swings.

MILLS

The club is held rather lightly between the thumb and first finger in order to allow for ease of manipulation, but though the grip is nowhere near as firm as that required for the swings, care must be taken to ensure that it is sufficiently tight to maintain contact throughout. A grip which is too loose can result in the club flying out of the hand – possibly causing damage.

In the learning stages, one club may be discarded, and the manipulations practised with one hand at a time. Start by holding the arm down in front of the body, and circle the club in the door plane, outwards first, then inwards. The technique involves a pivot action of the head of the club between the thumb and first two fingers rather than a circling action of the wrist, which means that the grip must not be too rigid. In trying to achieve the correct technique, imagine that it is the club which is doing the work, and not the wrist. Change hands frequently so that practice is gained with the left hand also, and then finally try the movement with a club in each hand, initially both clubs circling in the same direction.

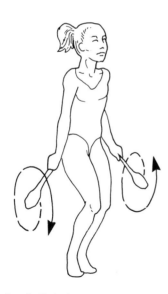

Fig 96   Small mills in the wheel plane.

Mill circles in the wheel plane are considered by some to be easier than those in the door plane, but that is for you to decide. The action is basically the same. The arm is held down at the side and the club rotated backwards or forwards at the side of the body. However, because of the position at the side of the body, the hand has to be turned outwards for the backward rotation, and more movement of the wrist is necessary. Similarly, for the forward rotation, a stronger action of the fingers is required to initiate the forward turn of the club. Unless the correct technique is adopted, it is difficult to keep the club in the correct plane: it should pass through a vertical position at all times, and should brush past the forearm on each upward circle. This is dependent to some extent upon a certain degree of flexibility and strength in the wrist joint and also the dexterity of the fingers.

Very much easier in the initial stage is the mill circle in the table plane. With the arm held out in front at shoulder height, palm facing downwards and the club hanging from the thumb and first two fingers, the wrist is gently circled and the club allowed to pivot between the fingers until it is circling in a horizontal position brushing just below the forearm. Here the circle is performed either inwards or outwards, with one or both hands and with both clubs going in the same or in opposite directions. If the latter, the arms need to be wider apart to avoid a clash of the clubs.

Other Moves using the Clubs

Other basic movements which are suitable for the beginner with clubs are those of tapping and rolling. Tapping (or beating) of the clubs adds to the rhythmic qualities of a routine (as does the bouncing of the ball) and it can highlight certain beats or pauses in the music. Use any part of the club: the body, the shaft or the head to beat the other club or to beat the floor.

Rolling the clubs on the body is becoming a popular skill nowadays, especially using an arm or a leg, but this requires a high level of handling skill because of the irregular shape of the club. On the other hand, rolling the clubs on the floor is simple and effective and is achieved by placing the clubs parallel on the floor and pushing the body of the clubs apart from each other in opposite directions. The clubs will roll in a curve through 180 degrees – an interesting movement when combined with a half turn in the kneeling position (lift the foot off the floor to allow the club to pass under it).

The more advanced movements of juggling and throwing do not come within the confines of this book. The skills are many and complex and require a thorough knowledge and understanding of the intricate techniques involved.

Sequences

Consideration can be given to the linking of simple swinging and circling movements with the clubs. Particularly effective is the *en masse* display where a number of gymnasts (the more the better, provided space allows) perform a series of simple large swinging movements in time with each other, perhaps choreographed to some suitable music which will both assist in the synchronisation and add to the entertainment. A good piece of music for this is the James Last version of 'Winchester Cathedral' – it provides an excellent rhythm and tempo for club swinging.

In devising individual sequences, consideration must be given to the inclusion of all types of elements both with apparatus and body, but it is equally, if not more,

important to build the sequence around the age and ability of the gymnast. It is far better to compose a routine which the gymnast can cope with and can perform well, than it is to compose one beyond her limitations. In a competition marks are lost each time a club is dropped, and, moreover, the composition becomes disjointed, undoubtedly showing a lack of harmony between the apparatus and body work. Changes of plane are also particularly important and must be evident, as well as the other factors concerned with general composition of an exercise.

CLASSWORK

Emphasis must be placed upon safety when working clubs with large numbers in the group. If there is insufficient apparatus to go round, then it is perfectly feasible for individuals to work with just one club each – in fact, this is probably more practical and beneficial in the early stages.

The coach must be aware of the amount of space that is needed for each of the exercises with the clubs. The swinging and circling skills obviously take up a lot of room, and if sufficient space is not available, then the class should be divided into two or more groups to practise these in turn.

The smaller mill circles can be trained on the spot, with little travelling by individuals, though once the basic manipulations have been achieved, they should be combined with suitable body elements. If you are venturing on to juggling or throwing, a floor covering such as a mat or a carpet serves several useful purposes: to help prevent breakage of clubs when dropped; to cut down the noise element created by dropped clubs; to protect the floor!

Partner work

The basis of partner work with clubs can be built upon simple matching movements performed in unison, and showing changing relationships between the two performers. The two clubs can be placed in one hand and passed to a partner as an exchange during a turn or a circling action of the arm, or they could be rolled or slid to each other within the composition of the sequence. There is more room here for originality and invention, allowing scope for the creative expertise of coach and gymnast.

8 Training

Though the sport of rhythmic gymnastics is fairly new, much progress has been made not just within the United Kingdom but also on the international scene. Through sheer hard work and determination (along with a training schedule which is very much part-time when compared to their Eastern Bloc counterparts) British gymnasts have raised their scores from the lowly 6.0s attained in their first World Championships in 1975, to the 9.0s which they are scoring today. However, it is becoming more apparent with the current standards of excellence at World and Olympic level that British gymnasts will be struggling even to maintain this level of work, let alone raise it further. The rigorous training programmes undertaken by such countries as Bulgaria and the Soviet Union are leaving many of the Western Bloc countries behind. Their systems of selection and priority training demand a sole, full-time commitment by gymnast and coach within a highly structured and well financed school. This, of course, is not the case in the United Kingdom, where it is difficult even to consider competing on the same level.

It is obvious that training is of vital importance for success at rhythmic gymnastics; everyone should improve their standard of performance if they follow a carefully structured schedule irrespective of their reason for taking up the sport and their reason for training.

REQUIREMENTS OF THE RHYTHMIC GYMNAST

The requirements of a successful rhythmic gymnast are many and varied, both physical and psychological. All of them need to be developed to the full, and all of them therefore should feature in the training programme to some degree. I list what I consider these attributes to be, though not in any special order of priority:

- Mobility and strength
- Co-ordination
- Musicality
- Elegance
- Expression
- Motivation

Mobility and Strength

The rhythmic gymnast has developed her own physical attributes quite unlike those of any other sportsperson. Of particular importance is mobility, especially in the spine, hips and shoulders. However, a high degree of strength is also necessary to control the very flexible movements which form an essential part of the work.

Strength is also required in the legs for the purpose of elevation in leaps and jumps; in the arms to assist throwing and manipulation techniques with the apparatus; and in the form of stamina for the explosive energy requirements of a full exercise. Indeed it would be impossible to over-emphasise the value of strength and mobility.

Fig 97   Mobility and strength are required for
          this balance.

Figs 98–99   The rhythmic gymnast requires the
              elegance of a dancer . . .

'Undoubtedly, the biggest deterrent to success in learning gymnastics skills is inadequate strength and flexibility. When students improve these qualities, they learn much more rapidly, and consequently with greater joy and satisfaction.'

(James Bailey, *Handbook of Gymnastics in Schools* (Allyn & Bacon, 1974), p. ix)

Every gymnast will have weaknesses in strength, in flexibility or in both, but should strive to improve their own physical condition, following a programme which could be quite individual and personal, much of which could be done at home in their own time.

Within this programme there must be incorporated both strength and mobility work – often a gymnast will work solely on her flexibility in order to increase the range

of movement, particularly if she is rather stiff, and the strength exercises tend to be forgotten. James Bailey (*Handbook of Gymnastics in Schools*, p. 45) even considers that strength is more important than anything else:

'Of all the components of motor fitness – strength, power, flexibility, agility, endurance, and balance – the most important single component is strength. Moreover it is most easily improved. Research has shown that an increase in strength does not cause a decrease in flexibility, endurance or balance. Increases in muscular endurance, speed, agility and power do result when strength is increased.'

For the rhythmic gymnast who needs such a high degree of suppleness in both the spine and the hip joint, I strongly recommend that

Fig 99

Figs 100–101   . . . and the expression of an actress.

the training programme pays particular attention to both the mobility and the strength components, for both are vital to this work.

Co-Ordination

It could be said that co-ordination is difficult to acquire – you either possess it or you do not. What is more correct, I feel, is that some people are better co-ordinated than others. The reasons for this are complex, but what must be understood is that co-ordination develops and improves with maturity and that practice, together with good coaching, can speed up and refine this development. Co-ordination is especially important in our sport for the gymnast as not only to be well co-ordinated in body movement, and in actions such as throwing, catching, and manipulating apparatus, but must be able to put all this together to produce a completely co-ordinated, stylish and elegant movement. Practice of body work and apparatus work, both separately and together, is essential if success is to be achieved.

Musicality

Like co-ordination, musicality is difficult to learn; indeed, I think it is true to say that people either possess a sense of rhythm or they do not. Certainly some people find it easy to tap out the beat of a catchy rhythm, and can dance to it quite sensitively but I am sure we have all also witnessed the person at the local disco who not only finds it hard to express the music, but cannot even keep in time with it. However, there are aspects of musical appreciation which can be trained, particularly with regard to the interpretation of certain rhythms and styles of music through appropriate movement patterns.

Fig 102   The gymnast should portray an air of elegance and beauty.

Elegance

If there is one thing rhythmic gymnastics is renowned for, it is surely elegance. Essentially a feminine sport, rhythmic gymnastics, despite its difficult and complex movement skills, portrays an air of beauty and maturity suggestive of an art-form. The elegance that is so inherently part of the 'sport' must be carefully nurtured during training. Indeed posture-training exercises, ballet and dance training, all play an important part in the gymnast's schedule.

However, to possess the correct physique for the sport is a much taller order – tall being the important issue: long legs, short body and a slim figure are all vital to success at the top level, but this must not deter anyone from participating in the sport, since the top level is for so very few.

Figs 103–104   Expressive performances.

Expression

To a very great extent this is dependent upon personality and so requires a special kind of development. The training required here is that of the theatrical performer. To be able to project oneself as if on stage, to give an expressive and meaningful performance, and at the same time satisfy the judges with the required elements is not at all easy, and requires more than a part-time training schedule!

It is hardly surprising that we cannot keep up with the top in the world, but then not everyone is expected to reach the top in the world. We can all achieve success at some level; we can all strive to improve our own level of performance and we can all enjoy participating in the sport. If we work to some sort of structured plan, then we are more likely to improve our fitness, and in consequence our level of skill.

Fig 104

Motivation

I use this term to encompass all the psychological and emotional requirements. The really dedicated gymnast will be totally committed to her sport, and want to do it to the exclusion of all else. From this commitment will come perseverance and this, together with concentration, will ensure that the gymnast will be well on the way to success. Without this desire to work, to perform, and to win, there is little chance of success, as Stuart and Sommerville (*Tackle Gymnastics* (Stanley Paul, 1980) p. 22) believe:

'Motivation is far more important than all the physical factors, for if the gymnast has the ideal physique but lacks the basic desire to be a good gymnast, the rest is worthless.'

They also believe that preparation is a vital ingredient for success:

'Good preparation leads to confidence and progressive success which satisfies and motivates further preparation etc. The magic word, however, is *preparation* – the greater the work put in at this point, the greater will be the rewards, and the stronger the motivation to further efforts.'

This preparation is essential in all aspects of the work, not just in the physical preparation of the body, but also in the planning of the training programme, the organisation and preparation of the facility, the apparatus, the music and all the other factors which play a part in the successful training session. This, along with a fully planned physical and psychological build-up to the competition or display is a pre-requisite for success.

PLANNING TRAINING

The amount and intensity of training will depend upon the aims of each individual and the circumstances which allow for those aims to be realised. Whether participation is purely for the promotion of health and fitness, or whether it is for entry into the competitive field, it is important to understand how to prepare and follow a specific training schedule. For beginners and young club gymnasts this would normally be done by the coach in charge. For the class in school this would of course be done by the teacher. Whatever the situation, there are bound to be restrictions within which the coach or teacher must work; of course this does not preclude any individual from working to their own schedule at home or even in their own facility, if available. Gymnasts should be encouraged to practise on their own in addition to the training time which can be provided for them, perhaps arranging for the use of the school hall or the local sports centre.

Frequency of Training

Newcomers to the sport might be introduced to a recreational class or club and attend once a week for an hour or more, but to reach any level at all, a minimum programme must consist of two training sessions a week, each session being of two or three hours duration. Naturally, any additional time spent training should produce better results. Ideally, with time available and with commitment from both gymnast and coach, training would occur six days a week, for five or six hours a day.

However much training is undertaken, certain precautions, for your own health, need to be taken. The following are the golden rules of training to which both gymnasts and coaches should adhere at all times:

1. Warm up thoroughly at the beginning of each session in order to prevent damage to muscles or joints.
2. Do some stretching exercises both before and after training, to increase and maintain the flexibility of your body.
3. Follow a sensible plan of work which promotes fitness and health and allows easier participation in the sport.
4. Take adequate rest and relaxation when not training so that the body can recuperate and regain energy.
5. Eat a sensible diet which will provide the necessary nutrients for an active life-style.

Follow these rules and you will reduce the likelihood of your injuring yourself.

Fig 106

Figs 105–107   Practice of the different ballet arm-positions and carriage from one to the other helps to develop a graceful line.

Content and Schedule

Each training session should follow a similar pattern, and time should be given to all of the various aspects, including:

1.	Body preparation:	warming up ballet and dance work stretching and suppling
2.	Technique:	body movement skills apparatus handling skills combined body and apparatus skills
3.	Sequence work:	Part and whole routines
4.	Conditioning:	Strengthening followed by stretching

91

Fig 107

The amount of time given to each part of the work in each session will depend upon the particular needs of the class or individual, and upon the short-term and long-term objectives. It will also depend to some extent on the number of training sessions held during the week: if there are several, more time might be spent on technique during one session and less on part or whole routines during another. Most coaches feel that there is never enough time available, so careful planning is essential to give a balanced programme and to get the best out of each gymnast when it is most needed.

TRAINING ACTIVITIES

Mobility

The aim is to increase the range of movement in the joints, and this requires a loosening of the joints and stretching of the muscles to allow a greater degree of movement. General stretching in the warm-up should be slow and controlled. Avoid any 'bouncing' or vigorous stretching as this could cause injury. Start with general stretching exercises and then follow with more specific mobility work.

Stretches: Shoulders

1. *Shoulder presses*. Kneeling on the floor, reach forwards with arms straight and press the palms and shoulders into the floor.
2. *Push backs*. Interlace the fingers and

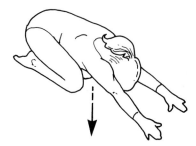

Fig 108   Shoulder presses.

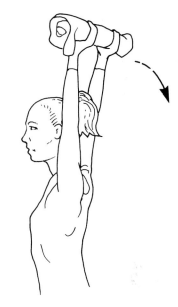

Fig 110   Towel push backs.

Fig 109   Push backs.

stretch arms above the head with palms
facing upward. Push the arms upward and
backward, keeping arms straight and head
up.

3.   *Towel push backs*. Holding a towel,
rope, or stick with both hands, stretch the
arms above the head, and back as far as
possible. Repeat, bringing the hands closer
together each time.

4.   *Bar presses*. With the feet slightly apart,
place both hands about shoulder width
apart on a bar or ledge and keeping arms

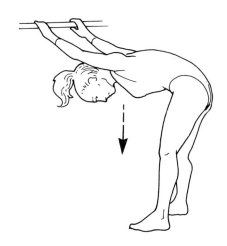

Fig 111   Bar presses.

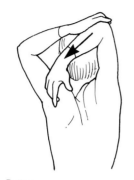

Fig 112 Pulls across.

Fig 114 Knee pulls.

Stretches: Hips and Legs

1. *Knee pulls*. Lying flat on your back, lift one leg and clasp the bent knee, pulling it into the chest as close as possible.
2. *Lunges*. Stand with one foot well forward, legs wide, and with the weight over the front bent leg, keep back leg straight and press both legs towards the floor. Support weight on the hands.

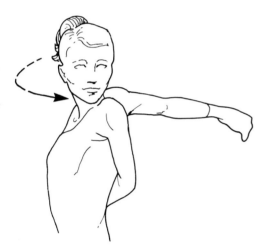

Fig 113 Wall stretches.

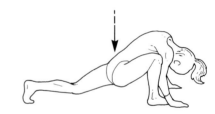

Fig 115 Lunges.

straight, press the shoulders down towards the floor.
5. *Pulls across*. Lift the arms overhead, bend one arm and catching hold of the elbow with the other hand, pull the arm across behind the head.
6. *Wall stretches*. Facing a wall, lift one arm sideways at shoulder height and place the palm, arm and shoulder against the wall. Turn the body away from the wall as far as possible, whilst keeping contact with the whole arm.

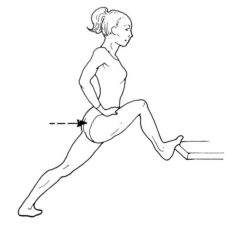

Fig 116 Bar stretches. (a)

(b)

5. *Straddle sits*. Sit on the floor with legs apart and back upright. Keeping your back straight, bend over one leg and press the ribs on to the thigh, first to the right, then left, then reach to the floor in the centre.
6. *Quads stretches*. Stand on one leg, and with the other knee bent, hold on to the foot at the back, and pull the leg backwards. Now try the exercise lying down.

3. *Bar stretches*. With one foot up on a bar, ledge or table, and keeping the supporting leg straight, first bend the lifted leg and push the hips towards the bar, then keep the leg straight and press the chest down on to it.

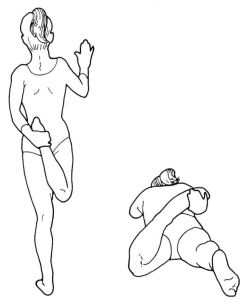

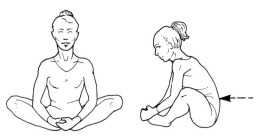

Fig 117   *Sole sits.*

Fig 119   *Quads stretches.*

4. *Sole sits*. Sit on the floor, and with knees bent place the soles of the feet together, then press both knees down towards the floor.

Stretches: Feet and Ankles

1. *Toe stretches*. Sit back on the heels, and keeping toes flat on the floor, lean backwards on to the hands so that the knees just come up off the floor.
2. *Ankle flexes*. Standing on one foot, hold the other leg out in front, just off the floor, point the toes and ankle towards the floor, then lift the foot up, toes pointing upwards.

Fig 118   *Straddle sits.*

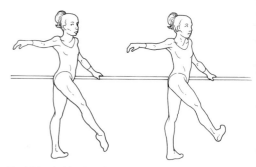

Fig 121   Ankle stretches.

Fig 120   Toe stretches.

3.   *Combined stretches*. Facing and holding a ledge or chair, stretch one foot to the side pointing the toes, then twist the foot in and place the heel down to stretch the back of the calf. On the next stretch, lean over the pointed toe and, bending the knee, turn the toes under.

Figs 122–124   Combined stretches for toes and ankles using further ballet exercises.

Fig 123

Fig 124

Training

Stretches: Fingers and Wrists

1. *Wrist circling.* Circle the wrists inwards, then outwards.
2. *Clenching and stretching.* Using a tennis ball, squeeze the fingers and hand around it. Relax a little and repeat, then open the fingers wide and straight so that the ball falls on the floor.
3. *Finger presses.* Interlace the fingers, turn the palms outwards and stretch both arms forwards pushing the fingers forwards.
4. *Wrist stretches.* Kneeling on the floor on all fours, with the fingers pointing back at the knees, palms on the floor, sit back towards the heels to stretch the front of the forearms and the wrists.

Stretches: Spine

1. *Side-bends.* Standing with feet slightly apart, stretch one arm overhead and bend to the side, change arms and bend to the other side, then repeat the side-bends with both arms overhead, and hands clasped.
2. *Trunk twists.* Standing with feet slightly apart and back to a wall, twist to one side and place both hands flat against wall.

Fig 125   Side-bends.

3. *Back arches.* Lying on the floor on your stomach, hands placed flat on floor under

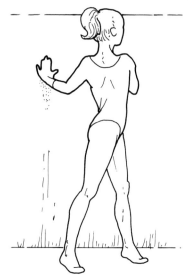

Fig 126   Trunk twists.

the shoulders, lift the shoulders and top part of body to arch the back, keeping hips on the floor.
4. *Bridges.* Lying flat on your back on the floor, with knees bent and feet flat on floor, lift hips off then lower. Next place the hands on the floor, and lift the hips and shoulders off.

Fig 127   Back arches.

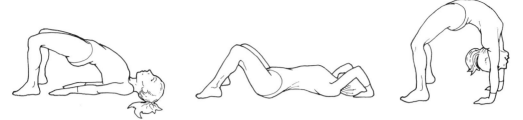

Fig 128   Bridges.

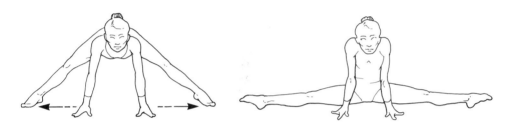

Fig 129   Box splits – straddle practice.

Fig 130   Box splits – chest flat to the floor.

Fig 131   Front splits practice

Specific Mobility Exercises

1.   *Box splits.* Practise standing in a straddle position (feet apart sideways) with legs straight. Place the hands on the floor, and gradually slide the feet further apart until sitting on the floor. Sit in box splits or as wide a straddle as possible, reach forward with the arms and get the chest flat to the floor.

2.   *Front splits.* Kneel on one knee, and stretch the other leg forward and straight. Place one hand on floor either side of the leg and gradually slide the leg further forwards. Sit in splits position, keeping both legs flat on the floor and hips square.

3.   *Walkovers.* Practise the bridge position from lying on your back, then lift one leg in the air. From a bridge position, kick over backwards through a back walkover, then practise a forward walkover from a standing position to land on one foot.

Constant practice will help to increase the suppleness and must be continued if flexibility is to be maintained. This is necessary even at the highest level, working alone or with partner assistance.

Strength

Stamina/Endurance

1.   *Jogging and sprinting.* If you go outside, jog on grass rather than a hard surface – it is kinder to the feet and ankles.

Figs 132–133   Examples of suppling work for the spine.

Fig 133

2. *Skipping.* Skip on the spot to music for ten minutes without stopping.
3. *Stairs exercise.* Run up and down stairs at least ten times.

Muscular Strength: Abdominals

1. *Abdominal curl.* Lie on your back with knees bent and feet on the floor, hands clasped behind the head, then lift the head and shoulders off the floor; build up the repetitions, starting with ten.
2. *Abdominal knee curl.* Lie on the floor, legs lifted and bent, arms clasped behind head and shoulders off the floor, touch left knee with right elbow, then right knee with left elbow; repeat five times each.

Muscular Strength: Back

1. *Back lift.* Lie on your stomach, hands clasped behind the head and partner holding the ankles down, then lift the upper body off the floor, at least ten times.
2. *Paddling.* Lying on your stomach, lift (straight) arms and legs off the floor, and paddle alternate leg and arm up and down.

Muscular Strength: Legs

1. *Step-ups.* Using a step, low chair or bench, step one foot up on to it and then the other; step back down with the first foot, then the second. Repeat at least twenty times.
2. *Leg lifts.* Standing on one leg, lift the other leg forwards and hold it for ten seconds.
3. *Sautés.* Small jumps on the spot with feet together. Do at least twenty, then stop and repeat.

Fig 134 Controlled leg lift to improve suppleness and strength.

Fig 135 Stretching with manual support, leg forwards.

Fig 138 Splits practice to improve suppleness in hips and legs.

Fig 136   Stretching with manual support, leg
sideways. Keep both legs straight.

Fig 137   Stretching with manual support, leg
backwards, slight lean forwards with
the shoulders and keeping the chest
and head up.

Fig 139   Suppling and stretching of spine together with splits practice.

Fig 140   The back-bend in use in a rope exercise.

Muscular Strength: Arms

1. *Press-ups.* Prone position, weight on hands and feet, and with body in a straight line, bend the arms and straighten as a normal press-up – build up the repetitions.

2. *Back press-ups.* With hands resting on a chair or bench behind the body which is stretched out forwards, bend and straighten the arms, as if performing a normal press-up, but facing up.

Fig 142   Partner stretching of shoulder joints.

Fig 141   Combined ballet and stretching exercise reaching full extension through spine and legs.

*Fig 143   Partner suppling of shoulder joint and stretching of hamstring
muscles.*

Fig 144   Partner suppling of legs and hip joint.

Fig 145   Individual exercises for stretching hip joints and spine.

Fig 146   Advanced partner stretching exercise – not recommended for
beginners.

Fig 147 Another example of a partner stretching exercise.

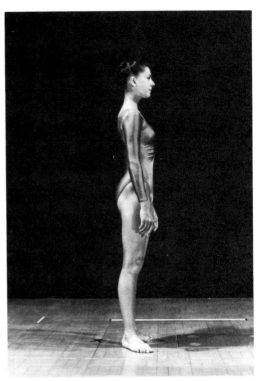

Fig 148 The plumb line should fall from the ear through the centre of the shoulder and down to the ankle bone.

Posture

1. *Back lying tension exercise I.* Practise lying flat on the back relaxed, then tighten all the muscles, stretching the arms and fingers to elongate the body.

2. *Back lying tension exercise II.* Repeat the above exercise, but concentrate on flattening the back into the floor, rather than elongating.

3. *Standing posture.* Practise standing correctly, with the stomach in, bottom in, shoulders down, arms relaxed at the sides. Then try this with a book balanced on your head.

Co-ordination

1. *Skipping.* With a rope, skip continuously incorporating changes of rhythm, speed,

direction of rope turn and footwork pattern.

2. *Throwing and catching.* First bowl (underarm) a tennis ball against a wall and catch the rebound, then throw a tennis ball overarm against a wall and catch the rebound. Throw a bean bag underarm into the air and then catch it again and finally practise the chest-pass with a large ball against the wall, catching the rebound.

3. *Bouncing.* Bounce a beach-ball, football or other large ball whilst standing, kneeling or sitting, then bounce a tennis ball around the leg or under the body.

4. *Rotating.* Practise rotating any size of plastic hoop first on the right hand, then the left and finally on both hands – in front, at the side and overhead.

Musicality

1. *Listen to music.* Play any music and identify style, rhythm and time signature, try to count, beat or clap in time to the music.
2. *Move to music.* Walk, run or jump in time to the music and try other body movements to express the music.
3. *Improvise.* Express the qualities and rhythms of a variety of styles of music, over-emphasise movement and expression and practise mime and facial expressions to suit the style of the piece of music.

Technique

Technique training involves the training for specific individual and combined skills of body and apparatus work. Training to improve mobility, strength, co-ordination, posture and musicality must go alongside technique training, for the one will aid the other. To quote Stuart and Sommerville (p. 11) again:

'Once the necessary preparation work has been done in each of the Ss of gymnastics, the learning of the skills is easy. Many gymnasts and coaches become frustrated through trying skills which they have not prepared for properly in one or more of these areas, often wrongly blaming the student's inability to learn.'

The Ss referred to above are, according to these authors, the requirements for a successful gymnast and although they are primarily concerned in their book with artistic gymnasts, interestingly they are very similar to the attributes which I suggested the rhythmic gymnast requires:

● Strength
● Suppleness
● Stamina
● pSychology

GOAL SETTING

Of importance to all athletes, whatever their sport, is a clear definition of aims and objectives. Each individual needs to know what he or she is working for, both in the long and the short term, and all training activities should be geared towards these overall objectives. These might be quite varied, according to the requirements of individual classes and gymnasts, perhaps including competitions, displays and awards tests on the one hand or purely experience, fitness training, or recreation on the other hand.

The coach will be the planner, the organiser, the teacher and the motivator and will be ready to adapt to the varying needs of the group in his or her charge. The approach for the highly competitive gymnast will, of course, be very different from the approach for the recreational gymnast – as will the level of work and the activities set. At a low level, to offer activities for the beginner, try some of the following:

Fun Activities

1. *Relays.* Teams of gymnasts could work up and down the hall: skipping with a rope; bouncing a ball; rolling a ball and jumping over it; rotating a hoop while running; rolling a hoop and jumping over it; skipping through the hoop.
2. *Obstacles.* Teams set an obstacle course which all members must complete and could include some of the following activities: bouncing a ball; skipping on the spot without tripping over the rope; getting through the hoop; bowling the ball to knock over skittles (clubs); holding a rope (folded

three times) in both hands and getting over it.

3. *Rope turns*. Two people turn a long rope (tie two or three ropes together) and gymnasts: run through; jump over and out; jump in, skip once, twice or three times, and then jump out; jump together into the rope and stay in.

4. *Partner activities*. These should include: matching and mirroring; over and under; copying; exchanges.

5. *Trio and group activities*. As above.

AWARDS SCHEME TESTS

Listed below are the skills on which individual gymnasts will be examined for their first awards badges. The BAGA scheme has recently been simplified and the work is aimed to encourage beginners to start on the right lines. These tests could form the basis of a training scheme, ensuring that all body elements are practised, and the fundamental apparatus techniques are learned and mastered. With the scope for so much variation in the work, the enlightened coach or gymnast will be able to develop the skills and add their own difficulty to the elements as progress is made.

Award 1

Free Exercise

Perform all six elements individually.

1. *Step*. Skipping step: four on the spot and four travelling forwards.

2. *Turn*. Three-step turn (a step to side right, half-turn right and step left, half-turn right and step to side right – 360 degrees completed). Repeat to left, on toes.

3. *Leap/jump*. Run forward and *jeté* leap, one foot to the other, *and* run and Komat jump.

4. *Balance*. Balance on one foot, other leg in any position, *and* balance on the bottom, legs in any position.

5. *Bend*. Kneeling on both knees, back-bend as far as possible.

6. *Wave*. Standing on both feet, perform a forward body wave with a ripple from feet up through body to head.

Rope

Perform all six elements individually.

1. *Skip*. On the spot, the rope turning forwards for twenty skips.

2. *Backward skip*. On the spot, slowly, for at least ten skips.

3. *Travelling skip*. One length of the hall, the rope turning forwards in half-time skipping (two steps for each rope turn – skip–step, skip–step).

4. *Open rope swing*. Swing rope forwards then back on the left side, the right hand into the left armpit, stepping back on to the left foot; swing the rope forwards, feet together, then back on the right side stepping back on to the right foot, the left hand into the right armpit.

5. *Folded rope swing*. Hold both ends of the rope in the right hand, perform helicopter-swings inwards overhead, change to the left hand overhead, swing left arm downward, pass rope behind the back to the right hand and lift to helicopter-swing inwards overhead (this should all be one continuous movement).

6. *Folded rope jump*. Fold rope into two or three, the ends held in each hand, and jump over the folded rope.

Training

Award 2

Free Exercise

Perform all six elements individually.

1. *Step.* *Chassé*-step travelling forwards (step forwards with the right foot, join the left foot to the right).
2. *Turn.* Push turn (step on to the right foot, then push with the left to turn 360 degrees to the right).
3. *Leap/jump.* Run forwards and stag-leap one foot to the other, *and* run forwards and perform a scissor-kick jump.
4. *Balance.* Balance on the toes of one foot with the free leg in any position.
5. *Bend.* Side-bend (standing with the weight on right foot and the left arm stretched upwards, bend sideways to the right and return to the start position, keeping head and arm together).
6. *Wave.* Kneeling on both knees, perform a wave/ripple from a curled position through the body to finish sitting up on the knees, arms stretched upwards.

Ball

Perform all six elements individually.

1. *Bounce.* Bounce the ball on the spot (two medium bounces, three quick bounces, so that the rhythm is 1–2, cha-cha-cha). Perform with the right hand and then the left.
2. *Bounce.* Bounce the ball on the spot with the right hand to the right of the body, and skip round the ball in a clockwise direction whilst bouncing. Repeat, switching hand, side and direction.
3. *Roll.* Roll the ball along the floor, run alongside and overtake the ball, then kneel down and collect it.
4. *Roll.* Roll the ball up both arms to the chest, and back down to the hands.
5. *Swing.* Swing the ball down and out to the right side and down and across to the left side, four swings with the feet apart, then repeat with the ball in the other hand.
6. *Throw.* Swinging the arm forwards and upwards, throw the ball with the right hand and catch the ball in both hands.

Award 3

Hoop

Perform all six elements individually.

1. *Rotation.* Rotate the hoop on the right hand between thumb and forefinger, arm stretched forwards and then walk backwards and forwards. Repeat on the left hand.
2. *Roll.* Roll the hoop along the floor, run beside it and perform a leap, then collect the hoop.
3. *Skip.* With the hoop turning forwards, skip several times through the hoop on the spot.
4. *Swing.* Holding the hoop in the right hand in undergrasp, swing it out to the right side, then pass overhead to the left hand and swing down. Repeat on the other side.
5. *Spin.* Spin the hoop on the floor, then run round it and collect it.
6. *Throw.* Throw with swing through from behind, with the hand in overgrasp, catch hoop and swing back. Repeat with right and left hand.

Ribbon

Perform all six elements individually.

1. *Snake.* Holding the stick in the right hand, work the wrist up and down whilst turning to the right. Repeat, turning to the left and with the ribbon in the left hand.

2. *Coil.* Make a stirring action with the wrist to make small circles with the ribbon, whilst running backwards.

3. *Figure of eight.* With the ribbon, first swing the right arm down and back on the left side and then on the right side of the body.

4. *Side swing.* Swing the right arm out to the side, down across and up to the left side, back out to the right and continue the circle up and overhead. Change hands overhead so that the ribbon ends up in the left hand.

5. *Side swing and turn.* Swing the right arm out to the right side with the ribbon in the table plane, then across to the left side, back across to the right side and then turn to the right. Circle the ribbon in the table plane, swing it across the body, finishing with the ribbon on the right side.

6. *Swing and snake.* Run forwards and swing the right arm forwards and upwards, then run backwards with the right arm stretched in front of you with the wrist working from side to side to show the horizontal snake pattern of the ribbon.

Appendix 1

APPARATUS SPECIFICATIONS

Measurements quoted are for full size senior equipment. Juniors and beginners are recommended to work with apparatus of lesser dimension and weight.

Apparatus may be of any colour, or mixture of colours, except gold, silver or bronze; nor may they be fluorescent.

Rope

Material hemp or any synthetic material which possesses similar qualities.
Length proportionate to the size of the gymnast – the ends reaching armpit level when standing on it.
Ends handles are not permitted but a knot may be tied at each end. Up to 10cm at each end may be covered with an anti-slip material.

Hoop

Material wood or plastic with smooth or ridged edge. May be covered partly or totally with adhesive tape.
Diameter interior diameter 80–90cm.
Weight minimum 300g.
Shape section may be circular, square, rectangular or oval.

Ball

Material rubber or synthetic material with the same elasticity as rubber.
Diameter 18–20cm.
Weight minimum 400g.

Clubs

Material wood or synthetic material. May be covered in part or in total by adhesive tape.
Length 40–50cm.
Weight minimum 150g per club.
Shape bottle shape. Wide part is the body; narrow part is the shaft; small knob at end is the head and has maximum diameter of 3cm.

Ribbon

Material satin or other unstarched material.
Weight minimum 35g (excluding stick or attachment).
Width 4–6cm.
Length minimum 6m finished length, one piece of ribbon. End attached to stick is double thickness for maximum length of 1m and stitched down both sides. Extremity may end in a loop or eyelet to permit attachment to stick.

Ribbon Stick

Material wood, bamboo, plastic or fibreglass. Bottom end may be covered with a non-slip material for a maximum of 10cm to form a handle.

Diameter Maximum 1cm at its widest part.
Shape cylindrical or conical.
Length 50–60cm including ring for attaching ribbon.

Attachment Maximum 7cm in length of cord, thread, metal pin or swivel, extending from end of stick. Maximum 5cm in length of whipping or binding to hold attachment in place.

Appendix 2

BRITISH CHAMPIONS 1976–89

Senior Individual Overall

1976	Elizabeth Mann	Leeds AI
1977	Sharon Taylor	Marsden GC
1978	Sharon Taylor	Marsden GC
1980	Sharon Taylor	Coventry & Bedford
1981	Sharon Taylor	Northampton RGC
1982	Frances Newman	Southampton AGC
1983	Jacqueline Leavy	Marsden GC
1984	Jacqueline Leavy	Marsden GC
1985	Lorraine Priest	Leeds AI
1986	Lorraine Priest	Leeds AI
1987	Alitia Sands	Coventry RGC
1988	Lisa Black	Northampton RGC
1989	Alitia Sands	Coventry RGC

Junior Individual Overall

1976	Estelle Clayman	Leeds AI
1977	Estelle Clayman	Leeds AI
1978	Lynette Gordon	Marsden GC
1980	Lorraine Priest	Leeds AI
1981	Michaela Walton	Northampton RGC
1982	Peta Machin	Northampton RGC
	Alitia Sands	Marsden RGC
1983	Alitia Sands	Coventry RGC
1984	Alitia Sands	Coventry RGC
1985	Nicola Waker	Marsden GC
1986	Kerry Assinder	Marsden GC
1987	Kerry Assinder	Marsden GC
1988	Joanne Rose	Coventry RGC
1989	Michelle Smith	Northampton RGC

Senior Team

1976	Chilterns GC
1977	Marsden GC
1978	Marsden GC
1979	Leeds AI
1980	Marsden GC
1981	Marsden GC
1982	Marsden GC
1983	Northampton MRGC
1984	Leeds AI
1985	Northampton MRGC
1986	Northampton RGC
1987	Northampton RGC
1988	Merseyside GC

Junior Team

1976	Leeds AI
1977	Leeds AI
1978	Marsden GC
1979	Marsden GC
1980	Marsden GC
1981	Marsden GC
1982	Northampton MRGC
1983	Marsden GC
1984	Northampton MRGC
1985	Northampton MRGC
1986	Marsden GC
1987	Marsden GC
1988	Coventry RGC

Under-11 Team

1985	PACE
1986	Coventry RGC
1987	Coventry RGC
1988	Coventry RGC

Glossary

Acrobatics Disallowed gymnastics skills of handstand, cartwheel and somersault.

Arabesque A balance position on one foot, other leg lifted high and straight at the back.

Arpeggios The notes of a chord on the piano played quickly one after the other, up and down the piano.

Attitude A balance position on one foot, other leg lifted high at the back, knee bent and at a higher level than the foot.

Bass Low sounding notes usually played on the piano by the left hand.

Body wave A rippling action through the body commencing either with the feet or the head.

Boxers Quick skips with a rope, jumping over the rope with each turn.

Canon In group work, gymnasts effecting a staggered movement in quick succession, i.e. one after the other.

Cat leap Jump from one foot to the other, knees bent high in front one after the other, also called a komat.

Chassé Three steps; step, close feet together, step – performed in any direction.

Code of Points Book of judging rules, with composition requirements, deductions for faults, and technical regulations.

Coils Pattern of small circles with the ribbon, made by a 'stirring' action of the wrist.

Door plane The area of space in front and behind the body through which movements of a vertical nature are performed, also known as the frontal plane.

Double skips Skipping with the rope turning twice for every jump of the feet.

First position Of feet; heels touching, feet turned out, as in ballet. Of arms; forwards at shoulder height, palms facing, curved shape.

Fish leap Jump from one or both feet with a back arch, one or both legs bending up towards the back of the head.

Frontal plane Technical term for door plane.

Group work Usually refers to six gymnasts working together in a group composition, but can involve duets and trios or larger groups for display work.

Half-shoe Rhythmic gymnastics slipper consisting of the front half of a shoe held in place by elastic around the heel.

Hamstrings The group of muscles at the back of the thigh.

Jeté A spring from one foot to the other: *petit jeté*; small spring, *grand jeté*; large jump.

Komat A jump from one foot to the other, knees bent up in front (also called a cat leap).

Leg lift Leg lifted straight – forwards, backwards or sideways – and held either 'independently' or with a hand grip.

Lunge Standing position, feet wide apart, one knee bent, other leg straight, forward or sideways position.

Mills Small wrist circling action with the clubs.

Pas de bas Scottish-dance style step pattern, springing 1–2–3.

Patter turn Turn on the spot with many little steps.

Phrase A passage of movement or music.

Pivot A spin turn (pirouette) on the ball of one foot.

Planes Areas of space around the body through which movement occurs, called the frontal, sagittal and transverse planes.

Plié Bending of the knee or knees, weight on one or both feet.

Pre-acrobatic Permitted gymnastics acrobatic elements such as rolls, splits, chest rolls.

Relevé A sharp rise up on to the toes of one foot.

Rotation Spinning of the hoop around hand, foot or other body part.

Sagittal plane Technical term for wheel plane.

Sauté Straight jump, large or small, from two feet and landing on two feet.

Scissors Jump from one foot to the other, swinging straight legs forwards and changing legs in the air with a scissors action.

Scrabble A tucked roll on the floor performed over one shoulder, part forward, part sideways.

Snakes Pattern of the ribbon showing folds like that of a snake in motion.

Spirals A circling or spiralling type of movement performed with either the body or the apparatus.

Split leap A forward leap from one foot to the other, showing a horizontal split position of the legs in the air.

Splits Sitting on the floor, legs split horizontally forwards or backwards, full length of both legs touching the floor.

Stag A jump from one or both feet showing a position in the air with the front leg bent and back leg straight.

Stutter Many quick little steps either on the spot or travelling a short distance.

Table plane Area of space around the body through which movements of a horizontal nature are performed, also known as the transverse plane.

Glossary

Tempo   A musical term referring to the speed of either the music or the movement.

Transverse plane   Technical term for table plane.

Treble   High sounding notes usually played on the piano with the right hand.

Unison   Movement by two or more people performed with complete synchronisation.

V sit   Sitting position with legs straight and raised in air, back straight, body forming a V position.

Walkover   Exercise of gymnastic agility arising out of a handstand and 'walking' through a back-bend on to one foot.

Wave   Rippling action of the body or arms, associated with a body wave.

Wheel plane   Area of space at either side of the body through which movements of a vertical nature are performed, also known as the sagittal plane.

Further Reading

Anderson, R., *Stretching* (Shelter Publications, 1980)

BAGA, *Awards Scheme (BAGA*, 1989)

BAGA Rhythmic Gymnastics Technical Committee, *Technical Booklets* (BAGA Technical Department, 1988). There are six of these booklets available

Bailey, J., *Handbook of Gymnastics in Schools* (Allyn & Bacon, 1974)

Beckman, M., *Jazzgymnastik* (KL Beckmans Tryckerier, Stockholm, 1966)

Bodo-Schmid, A., *Modern Rhythmic Gymnastics* (Mayfield Publishing Company, 1976)

Bott, J., *Modern Rhythmic Gymnastics* (EP Publications Limited, 1981)

Cochrane, T. S., *International Gymnastics for Girls and Women* (Addison Wesley, 1969)

Cohan, R., *The Dance Workshop* (Allen and Unwin, 1986)

Gleeson, G., *The Growing Child in Competitive Sport* (Hodder & Stoughton, 1986)

Hessel, S., *The Articulate Body* (St Martin's Press, 1978)

Lemaître, O., *Your First Book of Ballet* (Angus & Robertson, 1978)

Stuart N. and Somerville A., *Tackle Gymnastics* (Stanley Paul, 1980)

RULE BOOKS

International Gymnastics Federation, *Code of Points* (FIG, 1989)
This title is available from the BAGA.

British Schools Gymnastics Association, *Rules and Regulations for Schools Rhythmic Gymnastics Competition* (BAGA, 1989)
This title is available from the British Schools Rhythmic Gymnastics Secretary (*see* Useful Addresses).

Useful Addresses

INFORMATION

Technical Administrator for Rhythmic
Gymnastics
British Amateur Gymnastics Association
National Sports Centre
Lilleshall
Nr Newport
Shropshire TF10 9NB

British Schools Rhythmic Gymnastics
Secretary
c/o 2 Holcot Leyes
Hillside
Rugby
Warwickshire
CV22 5SJ

SUPPLIERS

For Music Cassettes

Ron Bentley
2 Winchester Road
Delapre
Northampton NN4 9AY

For Apparatus and Clothes

Carita House
Stapeley
Nantwich
Cheshire CW5 7KJ

C & G Davies & Son
17 Ludlow Hill Road
West Bridgford
Nottingham NG2 6HD

For Apparatus Only

Newitt & Co. Ltd
Claxton Hall
Malton Road
York YO6 7RE

Index

Index